Mayan Cuisine

Recipes from the Yucatán Region

Mayan Cuisine

DANIEL HOYER

PHOTOGRAPHS BY MARTY SNORTUM

Gibbs Smith, Publisher
TO ENRICH AND INSPIRE HUMANKIND

Salt Lake City | Charleston | Santa Fe | Santa Barbara

First Edition
12 11 10 09 08   5 4 3 2 1

Text © 2008 Daniel Hoyer
Photographs © 2008 Marty Snortum except as noted on page 216

Published by
Gibbs Smith, Publisher
P.O. Box 667
Layton, Utah 84041

Orders: 1.800.835.4993
www.gibbs-smith.com

Designed by Dawn DeVries Sokol
Printed and bound in China

Library of Congress Cataloging-in-Publication Data
Hoyer, Daniel.
  Mayan cuisine : recipes from the Yucatan region / Daniel Hoyer ;
photographs by Marty Snortum. — 1st ed.
    p. cm.
  Includes index.
  ISBN-13: 978-1-4236-0131-9
  ISBN-10: 1-4236-0131-9
  1. Maya cookery. 2. Cookery—Mexico—Yucatán (State) I. Title.

TX716.M4H72 2008
641.5972'65—dc22
                    2007033541

This book is dedicated to the millions of Maya cooks, both past
and present, who have contributed to the development of this diverse,
multifaceted, and ever-evolving gastronomic tradition.

Contents

Acknowledgments

I would like to thank the many people, too numerous to list here, that have guided me on my journey of discovery into the mysterious and unfamiliar world of Maya cookery and culture. I hope that my work has honored your gracious efforts to inform, edify and put up with a crazy gringo and his quest. Marty, Harriet, and Beto, thank you, for your creative efforts and your ability to translate my cooking and ideas into beautiful photography that without, few would even glance at my writing. Thank you also to Gini and Marty for lending me some of your Maya art for the book.

Many thanks also to Nancy and Tristan for your support, tolerance and eagerness to sample my attempts to master this style of cooking. Ian, your spirit continues to inspire and comfort me. Peace.

Introduction

WHO EXACTLY ARE THE MAYA? That question has puzzled explorers, anthropologists, archeologists, mystics and historians for centuries. Myth has been woven together with fact and romanticized to suit the needs, beliefs and hopes of the individuals describing this enigmatic ancient civilization and culture that continues to persist in an evolved but less dominate form evident in present-day society.

In the Archaic era, 6000 to 2000 B.C., the earliest villages appeared along the seacoast of the Caribbean and the development of efficient food collecting skills and rudimentary cultivation techniques allowed for a growing population that resided in permanent settlements.

The Preclassic era, 2000 B.C. to 200 A.D., heralded the beginnings of formal civilizations throughout Mesoamerica, most notably the Olmec of the Gulf Coast of present-day Mexico and the Chavin from the Andes in South America. Religion and complex economies began to emerge as a driving force in these societies that served as a model for future organization of culture and proliferation of concentrated settlements. The Maya civilization is first evident as an identifiable subset of Mesoamerican indigenous peoples in the Late Preclassic period, which lasted from 300 B.C. to 200 A.D. The range of Maya civilization eventually extended from the Yucatán peninsula in the north to present-day Honduras, Belize and Guatemala in the south and as far west as Chiapas and Tabasco.

The Classic Period, A.D. 200 to 900 is often referred to as the Golden Age of the Maya. During this time, the political structure became very powerful with armies and hereditary rulers and the Maya began to develop their own unique style and culture. Architectural masterpieces were created; religion became the center of the society, a written language was developed and complex agricultural systems allowed for ever-increasing populations. During this time, the ruling Jaguar dynasty of the Rio Usumacinta cities of Yachilan and Bonampak were dominant.

The Post Classical period, from A.D. 900 to 1500, saw the decline and eventual collapse of the strong Maya states. This era saw the abandonment of many sites along with the brief flourishing of new locations such as Uxmal and Chichen Itza in the Yucatán.

The Spanish Conquest of the Maya people occurred in 1541; however, many groups resisted and there have been a number of uprisings of note in recent history. The Maya are credited with compiling a complex and remarkably accurate calendar and the building of many spectacular edifices, some of which are just beginning to be discovered by archeologists.

Despite many hardships, repressions, disease and politics beyond their control, the Maya are a resilient people and the Maya culture is evident if not dominant in the regions that their ancestors settled and developed. The Maya language has fractured somewhat over time, although the many variations are still spoken today throughout the area.

Maya cooking is still practiced today; however, it now exhibits influences from Mediterranean Europe, the Middle East and the rest of Mexico and North and South America. The ancient Maya perfected the growing and cooking of corn, beans, squash, cacao, chiles and tomatoes to name a few of the better-known indigenous crops. Modern-day Maya cooking continues to utilize these New World staples along with the meats, spices, fruits, vegetables and cooking methods that their conquerors and recent immigrants, most notably the Christian Lebanese that begin arriving in the late nineteenth century to avoid persecution in their homeland, have contributed. In the early twentieth century, the wealth of the region increased dramatically due to the henequen, or sisal, plant that was used for rope and textile production around the world. This brought sophistication to the cooking of the area due to the increased trade and social exchange with Europe and North America. The Yucatán peninsula was geographically isolated from the main part of Mexico, encouraging more exchange with Europe than the rest of Mexico, resulting in an even greater influence on the cooking. One of the more notable examples of this is the continuing popularity of Dutch cheeses throughout the Yucatán. The Maya have always been quick to adapt new flavors and techniques into their unique style of cooking.

There is no way to separate the original indigenous cooking of the Maya from its modern expression, although the historical contributions are readily apparent. Mexican influences also abound but the unique Maya style is noticeable even in the preparation of classic Mexican recipes. Like its first cousin, Mexican cooking, Maya cuisine revolves around corn. Tortillas, tamales, atoles and numerous corn masa–based snacks abound. Squash and beans also figure prominently and the use of recados, ground seasoning pastes unique to Maya cooking, can be found in most recipes. Chiles, many unique to the region, are freely used in the cooking and the use of leaves to wrap food before cooking remains a practice. Besides corn, which is used in most indigenous cooking of the Americas, achiote, the paste made from the seeds of the native annatto tree, is the most identifiable ingredient in much of Maya food preparation.

Whether you are traveling through Maya lands or cooking Maya recipes in your home, you will enjoy the fresh, bold flavors and subtle sophistication of this celebrated, historic and often misunderstood style of cooking.

The recipes in this book are a compilation of my experiences in traveling and cooking in the land of the Maya combined with adaptations of some historical dishes. They are not intended to be an absolute treatise on the entire repertoire of Maya food; merely one person's experience and expression of this fascinating cooking style that encompasses many regional variations and customs. However, I do feel that it provides a window into the soul of Maya culture through its cooking and is an effective starting point for further exploration of a deep and complex cuisine. Many readers will be satisfied with learning some new recipes and flavors while some are more focused on tradition and history. All are welcome to experience and experiment.

¡Buen Provecho!

Daniel Hoyer

Ingredients and Techniques

The Mexican Way of Cooking

IN A PERFECT WORLD, all of the ingredients for a given recipe would be readily available, in wonderful peak condition and of uniform flavor; however, that is not always the case. In reality, the item called for may be out of season, not at its peak of ripeness or just not convenient to obtain. Also, fresh food varies from plant to plant and region to region. Two chiles from the same plant may range from mild to fairly hot; normally tame poblano chiles may sometimes be fairly hot due to the season or where they were grown and diverse varieties of tomatoes have different flavors; some are sweet, some are more acidic. Dried herbs and spices may also lose some intensity of flavor over time depending on how they have been stored.

To cope with these challenges, cooks need to be flexible and use their taste buds along with their experience and a little intuition. A recipe provides a guideline that often needs interpretation and some adjustment. Along with the previously mentioned variations and occasional lack of availability, good cooks also like to express their own personal style by varying recipes and substituting ingredients to suit their personal tastes and to please their guests.

In Mexico—and the Maya world is no exception—many traditional recipes use terms like *bastante* (enough or sufficient) or *cocinar muy bien* (fry or cook well) and *al gusto* (as you like). The amounts given are often very ambiguous, allowing for the cook's own interpretation and to accommodate what is available, particularly since many rural areas and small villages have limited resources, and depend upon seasonal ingredients. I encourage you to take liberties with the recipes in this book. I have sometimes listed logical replacements for ingredients based on my tastes but you should feel free to make substitutions, as you like. You may prefer spicier or milder, jalapeño chiles to habanero chiles, more or less onions and garlic, sea bass instead of snapper, and so on. Please feel free to make the recipes your own. There is no right or wrong to great cooking if the results please the cook and his or her guests.

Sour Oranges

The sour oranges, or *naranjas agrias*, of the Yucatán peninsula are at this time very difficult to find outside of that area. Although they are an essential component of the flavors of present-day Maya cooking, they can be approximated with some success. Mixing sweet orange juice with mild vinegar like apple cider or rice vinegar or by combining lime juice, sweet orange juice and sometimes a little grapefruit juice works pretty well for me. It is not an exact substitute but does fit into most recipes that call for sour orange juice. Frequently asking the produce department of your favorite store for sour oranges may also help to motivate the fruit suppliers to start to bring them in.

Sautéing or Frying

Sautéing is another way of exposing ingredients to high temperature to produce flavors, texture and color. Many restaurant cooks as well as home cooks often get this wrong. Do not be afraid of the high setting on your stove when sautéing or frying. If you want to reduce the mess from splattering, you can use a high-sided pan or a splatter screen.

My rule of thumb is "Hot pan, cool oil (or fat)." The pan needs preheating to ensure that there is enough heat before adding the room-temperature oil. This will also cause the food in the pan to stick less. Keep the temperature high and only reduce the heat if things start to burn. Do not overload the pan. Many meats and vegetables contain a large amount of liquids and an overly full pan will not maintain enough heat to achieve the desired results. Also, stirring cools down what you are cooking so keep the stirring to a minimum, especially at the beginning.

Toasting Onions

In Maya cooking many recipes for salsas, sauces and broths call for toasted onions. Toasting sweetens the onions, removing or reducing the "hot" taste of raw onions. Slightly charring the onions will also produce flavor that is complementary to roasted chiles, tomatoes and tomatillos.

On a preheated comal or heavy skillet or a baking sheet in a 350-degree-F oven, place slices or quarters of onions and roast, turning occasionally, until a golden brown color develops (a little black around the edges is okay).

Toasting Garlic

Garlic cloves are toasted whole to remove the raw taste and to sweeten the flavor. Toasted garlic is more subtle in flavor so you usually will need to use more than if you are using the garlic raw. Peeled garlic will roast quicker and develop a darker color. Unpeeled cloves tend to get sweeter when toasted and stay lighter in color. If the recipe does not specify, the choice is yours. I use both methods depending on the flavor I want.

Garlic is toasted like onions and the two may be done together. They require the same temperature; however, the timing may differ. Unlike in Italian recipes, toasted garlic in Maya cooking is roasted at a higher temperature for a shorter time; therefore, it does not get as soft and mushy. Some firmness remains.

Tamale Wrappers

Most tamales are wrapped either in dried cornhusks or in banana leaves. If you cannot find one of these you can always substitute the other. Dried cornhusks need to be soaked before using to make them pliable. Place the husks in a bowl or pan deep enough to submerge the husks and add enough water (hot water speeds the process) to completely cover. Soak for at least an hour and up to overnight. When using, make sure to drain and wipe off the excess water.

Banana leaves may be found in Mexican and Latin groceries or Asian markets, usually frozen. To use, thaw first, then rinse well and wipe dry. With a scissors or sharp knife, cut into pieces appropriate for the recipe that you are using. The leaves need to be lightly toasted before filling to make them pliable and to prevent splitting. Toast over a direct flame or on a comal for a few seconds. You will notice the color of the leaf changes slightly as heat is applied. The surface of the banana leaf will develop a shiny quality as it is toasted. Do not overtoast, as this will cause the leaf to be brittle. Cover the toasted leaves with a damp towel until you are ready to use them.

ROASTING, TOASTING AND CHARRING

Fire is an indispensable element in Maya/Mexican cookery. It is used with a comal or skillet to unlock the flavors of dried chiles, herbs and other spices; and with tomatoes, tomatillos, garlic and onions to enrich the taste through caramelizing and charring. Fresh chiles, tomatillos and tomatoes are often roasted over an open flame or directly on hot coals to impart an even more intense smokiness. The extra flavor and complexity achieved by roasting and toasting can be useful to many styles of cooking, not only Maya/Mexican. This application of intense heat also reduces the overall cooking times for many recipes, as a long simmering time is often unnecessary for full flavor development. If you learn only one new technique from this book, this is the most important. It can improve the flavors of all of your cooking.

Dry Spices, Chiles and Herbs

Preheat a comal, heavy skillet or Dutch oven over a medium-high heat until you can feel the heat radiate from the surface (the surface should be 350 to 375 degrees F). Toast the coarser items like whole chiles and seeds first, followed by herbs and leaves. Finish with ground spices and lastly with ground chiles. Finely ground spices have more surface area exposed to the heat so they are more likely to burn. You will want to finish quickly as the chile smoke is irritating and may cause you to cough and sneeze. Ventilate well. Stir or toss frequently to allow even toasting; you want to lightly char, not scorch, the ingredients. When some smoke appears and color begins to develop, remove to a cool container or surface. Make sure to wipe out the pan before adding a new ingredient. You do not want to burn the remaining particles from the previous toasting. Only toast what you can use in your day's cooking. Toasting releases the flavors and by the next day there will not be much left.

Delicate "sweet" spices like canela (cinnamon) and cloves have such a volatile flavor that toasting can cause a loss of flavor. I toast allspice when used in savory dishes and not when used in a sweet dish.

Whole seeds may be ground in a mortar and pestle, spice grinder or molcajete immediately after toasting. Herbs are usually added whole but sometimes are also ground.

Soaking Toasted Dried Chiles

Before or after they are toasted, dried chiles are usually stemmed and seeded, and then soaked in very hot (180–200 degrees F) water for 15 to 20 minutes to rehydrate them. Remove them from the soaking water by using tongs so that any grit that has settled to the bottom of the water is not mixed back on to the chile. Do not soak for longer than 20 minutes as the flavor will be diminished.

Fresh Chiles

Fresh chiles are fire-roasted to remove the skin, begin the cooking process and to give them a smoky and slightly sweeter flavor. The larger varieties like poblano, New Mexican green and Anaheim are usually roasted and peeled. The smaller types like jalapeño, serrano and habanero may be used raw or roasted and charred and then peeled and seeded (or left intact) for some sauces and salsas. This method also works for sweet bell peppers (chiles dulces).

Place the chile over a direct flame or as near to a direct source of intense heat as possible (open gas burner, charcoal or gas grill, oven broiler or toaster oven) and char the skin until at least 80–90 percent of the skin is blistered and blackened. Rotate often to cook evenly. Place in a paper or plastic bag or in a bowl covered with a kitchen towel or plastic wrap to trap the steam. This will loosen the skin and continue cooking the chile. After 10 to 15 minutes, rub the chile surface with a cloth or paper kitchen towel to remove the skin. I *do not* recommend rinsing in running water to remove the skin. Although that method is very efficient, the water also removes much of the flavor that you have been working so hard to create. After peeling, the chile may be carefully slit open on one side to remove the seeds before stuffing for chile rellenos, or the stem and seeds may be removed prior to chopping to use in salsa or to puree for a sauce or soup.

You may want to wear surgical or rubber gloves when handling the chiles to avoid burning your skin. Always remember to wash your hands well after peeling chiles; if you forget and touch yourself, you may regret it. A vinegar rinse followed by soap and warm water works well.

Tomatoes and Tomatillos

Both tomatoes and tomatillos may be toasted or charred to improve their flavor for salsas, sauces and soups. They may be flame-charred, roasted directly on coals or pan-roasted on a comal or well-seasoned skillet or on a baking sheet in a 350-degree-F oven for a sweeter, more concentrated, flavor. Pan-roasting may also be used to blacken the fruits if you desire. This method also produces a more pronounced ripe flavor—useful for those almost flavorless, pink, winter tomatoes.

Tomatillos need to be husked before roasting. Some soak them to loosen the skin and remove the sticky substance from beneath the skin. I prefer to husk them dry and then rinse in very warm water for a few seconds to remove the stickiness.

For flame-roasting, proceed as with fresh chiles until the desired degree of blackness is achieved. If you are using a pan or comal, preheat to about 325 degrees F and place the tomatoes and/or tomatillos in the dry pan over a medium-low to medium heat. (The pan or comal should be well seasoned but do not add oil. You are roasting, not frying.) Turn occasionally but not too often. Remove from heat when blackened or browned as desired and chop or puree as needed.

Recados

UNDERSTANDING AND MASTERING recados is one of the most important keys to achieving the distinctive flavors of Maya cooking. Recados are utilized as seasoning rubs and marinades, added to tamales, and often used to flavor sauces, soups and stews. The term *Recado* or *Recaudo* has several meanings in Spanish, ranging from messenger to safekeeping. In the Maya territories, the term almost always refers to seasoning pastes used every day and for special occasions like fiestas. When employed for cooking, I suppose that you could say that the Maya recados are flavors in safekeeping and that they are messengers of tastes from the ancient past. The Maya have used recados for millennia; however, the arrival of the Spanish most certainly enriched the ingredients used and the variety of flavors achieved. Recados were a convenience food for the ancient Maya of the Yucatán and the gulf coast of Campeche; these premade, savory concoctions are unique to Mexican cooking; no where else in the country

are spice mixtures commonly prepared in advance and employed on a daily basis as part of the regular cooking routine.

Most recados are a blend of herbs, spices, at times chiles, and other seasonings, frequently with the brick-red achiote or annatto seed included. They are typically made ahead of time and their use simplifies the preparation of meals. If well wrapped, most recados will keep up to one year in the refrigerator or they may also be frozen.

The following recipes are characteristic examples of the infinite number of recados found in the cooking of the Maya world and will serve you well for most Maya recipes. You will notice that there are a lot of similarities between many of the recados that follow. A native Maya would insist that these are distinct differences; however, you should feel free to use any recado that you have on hand that is similar to what is called for in a recipe, as the results will still be good.

Recado Colorado

Red Seasoning Paste

RECADO COLORADO IS THE MOST COMMONLY USED of the recados in Maya cooking. It is used to season meats, poultry and seafood before cooking and as a flavoring and colorant for sauces and tamales. Many recipes in this book call for it. Achiote paste is readily available in markets and groceries in both the United States and Mexico, and the store-bought version, usually labeled *Condimento de Achiote,* is quite serviceable (I use it a lot), but at times it is gratifying to create the distinct flavors of the homemade variety and to control the subtle tastes oneself. The annatto seeds are pretty tough. If you do not have a molcajete or a very powerful spice grinder, I recommend using pre-ground annatto seeds or just stick to the commercially prepared recado.

Makes about 8 ounces

1. Mix the annatto seeds with the 2 tablespoons of vinegar and soak for several hours (if using pre-ground seeds, proceed to the next step without the soaking).

2. Finely grind all of the ingredients in a molcajete or durable spice grinder.

3. Mix until a smooth, stiff paste is formed, adding more vinegar as needed.

4. Form into a block or in circular discs, wrap well and refrigerate to store.

1/2 cup annatto seeds (achiote) or 1/3 cup ground annatto seeds

2 tablespoons, plus more as needed, apple cider vinegar

8 whole allspice berries, lightly toasted

1/2 teaspoon coriander seeds (optional), lightly toasted

2 teaspoons whole black pepper

1/2 teaspoon cumin seed, lightly toasted (optional)

4 to 5 whole cloves (optional)

12 to 14 cloves garlic, roasted and peeled

1 tablespoon Mexican oregano, lightly toasted

1-1/2 teaspoons salt

Chilmole o Recado de Relleno Negro
Black Seasoning Paste

12 to 16 chiles Ancho (mild), mulato (medium) or guajillo/New Mexican red (hot) chiles (or a mix of all), toasted nearly black, stemmed and seeded

OR

6 ounces Chiles Secos de Yucatán, toasted nearly black, stemmed and seeded

1/4 cup annatto seeds (achiote) or 3 tablespoons ground annatto

2 tablespoons, plus more as needed, apple cider vinegar

2 corn tortillas, toasted on a comal or griddle or char-grilled until black

8 whole allspice berries

1 (2-inch-long) stick canela

2 teaspoons whole black pepper

6 whole cloves (optional)

20 cloves garlic, peeled, toasted and smashed with the side of a knife or kitchen mallet to form a paste

1 medium white onion, sliced in thirds, pan-toasted and finely minced

2 tablespoons Mexican oregano, lightly toasted

3 to 4 leaves fresh epazote (optional)

2 teaspoons salt

THIS DARK-BLACK, SHINY AND FLAVORSOME PASTE is used for both everyday cooking and for special occasions, as well as fiestas. The word *chilmole* comes from the Náhuatl word for chile sauce and hints at the influences from the Aztecs of central Mexico and other indigenous groups like the Zapotecas and Mixtecas from Oaxaca. The optional ingredients are usually added when a celebration warrants the extra expense resulting in the Relleno Negro version that is most notably a part of the special occasion dish Pavo en Relleno Negro (see page 158). To get the complete authentic flavor found in the Yucatán, you will need the chiles secos only available in markets there, but the other chile choices listed in the recipe make a very suitable substitute. I usually use a blend of all three of the optional varieties when I make it at home. In Maya territory, the chiles are often burned with flames created by adding dry cornhusks or alcohol to the hot comal along with the chiles to facilitate the blackening; however, I find that a deep charring on the comal or in a heavy skillet produces the desired results without as much drama, nuisance or peril.

Makes about 16 ounces

1. Soak the charred chiles in hot water for 10 to 15 minutes, drain and then rinse them thoroughly in cool water.

2. Mix the annatto seeds with the 2 tablespoons of vinegar and soak for several hours (if using ground annatto continue to the next step without soaking and reserve the vinegar for the paste blending).

3. Finely grind all of the dry ingredients in a molcajete or durable spice grinder.

4. Mix all of the ingredients in a molcajete or blender until a smooth paste is formed, adding more vinegar as needed.

5. Form into a block or in circular discs, wrap well and refrigerate to store.

Recado de Bistec
Herbal Seasoning Paste

THIS PEPPERY RECADO is not only used for beef recipes, as the name implies, but is commonly called for in preparations of pork, chicken and seafood. The deep herbal, spicy flavor and light green color are a nice alternative to the achiote-based recados. In addition to the traditional uses, you may enjoy this seasoning as a marinade for grilled food and as an additional flavoring in vegetable dishes and soups.

Makes about 4 ounces

1. Finely grind all of the dry ingredients in a molcajete or durable spice grinder.

2. Mix until a smooth, stiff paste is formed, adding vinegar as needed.

3. Form into a block or in circular discs, wrap well and refrigerate to store.

2 teaspoons coriander seeds

1 tablespoon whole allspice berries

1 (1-inch-long) stick canela

2 tablespoons whole black pepper

1 teaspoon whole cloves

Pinch cumin seed

12 cloves garlic, pan-toasted and peeled

1 tablespoon Mexican oregano, lightly toasted, OR 2 tablespoons fresh oregano leaves

4 to 5 leaves fresh epazote leaves (optional)

2 teaspoons salt

Apple cider vinegar, as needed

Recado de Escabeche

Seasoning Paste for Vinegar-Based Dishes

1 (2-inch-long) stick canela

10 to 12 whole cloves

6 whole allspice berries

1-1/2 teaspoons oregano

2 tablespoons black peppercorns

1/2 teaspoon cumin seed

1/2 teaspoon salt

3 to 4 bay leaves (optional)

12 cloves garlic, toasted and peeled

1/2 medium white onion, sliced
   1/4 inch thick and pan-toasted
   until charred around the edges

1 to 2 teaspoons apple cider vinegar,
   as needed

ESCABECHE CAN MEAN pickled or a method of cooking foods like seafood or poultry along with a sauce containing vinegar and spices. This recado may be used in both cases, as well as for seasoning soups and stews.

Makes about 6 ounces

1. Finely grind all of the ingredients except garlic, onions and vinegar in a molcajete or durable spice grinder.

2. Puree the onion and garlic in a blender with some of the vinegar to make a smooth paste.

3. Add the ground spices and mix until a smooth, stiff paste is formed, adding more vinegar as needed.

4. Form into a block or in circular discs, wrap well and refrigerate to store.

Salpimentado
Peppery Seasoning Paste

THIS RECADO IS A BASIC blend of seasonings that may be used to flavor salsa, soups and stews or rubbed on meat or poultry before roasting or broiling. Its name, which means salt and pepper, would lead you to believe that salt is a part of the paste, but it is not added until the recado is used.

1. Peel the onion and roughly chop along with the garlic. Puree in a blender until smooth.

2. Finely grind the pepper, canela, cloves and oregano in a spice grinder or molcajete.

3. Combine everything in the blender and puree until well mixed.

4. Form into a block or a circular disc, wrap well and refrigerate to store.

1 medium white onion, pan-toasted until charred around the edges (leave the peel on while toasting)

12 cloves garlic, toasted and peeled

1-1/2 tablespoons whole black peppercorns

1 (1-inch-long) stick canela

1 teaspoon whole cloves

1 tablespoon fresh oregano leaves or 1-1/2 teaspoons lightly toasted Mexican oregano

Recado de Especie o Mechado
Spice Seasoning Paste

FOUND IN SOUTHERN QUINTANA ROO and Northern Belize, these two recados are almost identical; Especie has the addition of saffron, making it a little pricier. The term *mechado* is in reference to the act of sticking or piercing; also, something that is used to pierce. I am not sure if that means the recado is stuck into the meat, or that it implies the flavor will pierce through to the meat. Both ways it is tasty and you can use it with or without the saffron.

Makes about 3/4 cup

1. Grind the dry spices to a fine powder.

2. Puree the onion and garlic in a blender, then add the ground spices and mix well.

3. Form into a block or a circular disc, wrap well and refrigerate to store.

1-1/2 tablespoons whole black peppercorns

1 (1-inch-long) stick canela

1/2 teaspoon whole cloves

1 teaspoon Mexican oregano

8 whole allspice berries

1/4 teaspoon cumin seed

2 generous pinches saffron (optional to make Recado de Especie)

1/2 medium white onion, sliced 1/4 inch thick and pan-toasted until charred around the edges

10 cloves garlic, toasted and peeled

Adobo Blanco o de Puchero
Seasoning Paste with Coriander

THIS RECADO IS PRETTY MUCH the same as de Especie, with the addition of coriander seeds and omitting the allspice, although you could certainly leave it in with good results. The name Adobo Blanco would seem to imply a white recado but it actually refers to the white sauce in which it is often used. Puchero is a type of stew and this recado is great for flavoring soups, stews and most vegetables.

Makes 3/4 cup

Follow the instructions for *Recado de Especie*, replacing the allspice berries with 1 teaspoon of coriander seeds.

Chilaquil
Seasoning Paste for Chile Sauces

THIS RECADO IS SOMEWHAT unique in that it has no canela and relies heavily on epazote for flavor. It is used to season chile sauces and, in Campeche and parts of the Yucatán, it is added to the masa or fillings in tamales. When combined with a chile sauce and strips of tortillas, it creates a Maya version of the ubiquitous Mexican dish, Chilaquiles.

1. Finely grind all of the dry ingredients first.

2. Add the garlic, herbs and liquids and mix to a smooth paste in a blender or molcajete.

3. Form into a block or a circular disc, wrap well and refrigerate to store.

1 tablespoon whole black peppercorns

2 teaspoons fresh oregano or marjoram leaves OR 1 teaspoon Mexican oregano, toasted

8 to 10 leaves fresh epazote

Generous pinch cumin seed

2 tablespoons finely ground annatto seed (achiote)

1 teaspoon salt

10 cloves garlic, peeled and coarsely chopped

3 tablespoons sour orange juice OR 2 tablespoons orange juice and 1 tablespoon lime juice

2 teaspoons apple cider vinegar

Adobo para Pato
Duck Seasoning Marinade

3 to 4 inches canela stick

Pinch cumin seed

1 tablespoon whole black peppercorns

1-1/2 tablespoons achiote or ground
annatto seed

1-1/2 teaspoons salt

1/2 onion, peeled, cut in two round
slices and toasted golden brown

6 cloves garlic, toasted and peeled

4 cloves raw garlic, peeled

1 tablespoon cider vinegar

1 to 2 tablespoons orange juice

ALTHOUGH INTENDED ESPECIALLY for duck, this marinade is excellent for turkey, chicken and game birds too. For duck, it is applied to the meat after partial cooking; the meat is then seared in hot oil or fat, then braised in a little broth until tender and the broth has reduced to a thick sauce. I also like to pre-marinade poultry with it, then slow roast or smoke the bird.

Makes about 2/3 cup

1. Finely grind all of the dry spices.

2. Add the onion, garlic and liquids and puree smooth.

3. Form into a block or a circular disc, wrap well and refrigerate to store.

Xak
Dry Spice Mix

2 teaspoons whole allspice

3 to 4 inches canela stick

1-1/2 teaspoons whole black peppercorns

1 teaspoon whole cloves

2 teaspoons Mexican oregano

Generous pinch cumin seed

2 teaspoons salt (the salt may be
omitted and added as needed
when the rub is used)

PRONOUNCED shăk, this dry rub or seasoning is found in markets, tiendas and supermarkets around the Yucatán peninsula. It is intended for poultry and I also like it on pork and in some fish dishes. Use it to season meats before grilling, sautéing and roasting or to flavor ground meats used as fillings, meatballs or burgers.

Makes 1/4 cup

1. Grind all the ingredients together until very fine.

2. Seal in an airtight container to store.

Recado de Alcaparrado
Seasoning for Caper Dishes

THIS SEASONING IS USED in Campeche and parts of the Yucatán for recipes including, as the name implies, capers and usually containing olives and raisins as well, expressing the Spanish influence in the Maya world.

Makes about 1/3 cup

1. Finely grind all of the dry spices.

2. Add the garlic and herbs along with the vinegar and puree to a smooth paste.

3. Form into a block or a circular disc, wrap well and refrigerate to store.

5 to 6 fresh oregano or marjoram leaves OR 2 teaspoons Mexican oregano

1 teaspoon coriander seed

1/2 teaspoon cumin seed

1 (2-inch-long) stick canela

1 tablespoon whole black pepper-corns

1/2 teaspoon whole cloves

1/2 teaspoon salt

8 cloves garlic, peeled and well smashed

Enough cider vinegar to moisten

Salsas

SALSA IS ONE OF THE FIRST THINGS that comes to mind when thinking about Mexican food, and the ever-present bowl of salsa, or frequently an assortment of spicy concoctions, is an important part of Maya gastronomy too. Whether they are used to flavor soups or stews, top antojitos, eggs or tamales, dress tacos or just to go with tortillas, salsas add that extra spark of flavor and heat that is important to the cuisine. Although the chiles that grow in Maya territory tend to be some of the hottest on the planet, they are used sparingly in most recipes, with the role of incendiary condiment reserved for the salsas that are customarily served on the side. This allows for accommodation of the wide array of tastes and tolerances for chile heat that is typical among families and guests,

even in this land where the chile is such an important part of the culture. Many of the day-to-day foods consumed in this region are rather basic and the addition of a tasty salsa can make an austere meal of corn atole, beans or tortillas much more appetizing and satisfying. The Maya have a saying, "A meal without chile, is no meal."

The salsas in this chapter all stand alone and have various uses, and many of them are also essential components of other recipes in this book. As in most cases in this style of cooking, the recipes serve as guidelines rather than rules, and you should feel free to make adjustments, to accommodate either your own or your guests' tastes or to adapt to the availability of ingredients.

Xnipec
Fresh Picante Tomato Salsa

1-1/2 cups diced ripe tomatoes
(about 4 to 5 Roma or
2 to 3 medium)

1 or 2 habanero chiles, stemmed,
seeded and finely chopped

1 medium (1/2 cup) red or white
onion, diced and rinsed (see
page 19)

4 tablespoons sour orange juice OR
3 tablespoons sweet orange juice
plus 1 tablespoon mild vinegar
OR 3 tablespoons lime juice

1/2 teaspoon or more salt, to taste

1/4 cup loosely packed, chopped
cilantro leaves

1 teaspoon vegetable oil (optional)

No COLLECTION OF RECIPES from this area would be complete without this salsa. It is to be had on nearly every restaurant table and is also served in the homes of the Maya world, especially in the tourist zones of the Yucatán and Quintana Roo. Pronounced Shnēē-peck, its name translates as "dog's nose," which should give you a hint about how hot it is. After consuming this sizzling concoction, all but the most jaded of chile heads are sure to have a wet nose and watery eyes from the fiery, yet complexly floral and fruity habanero chile. If you are concerned about the heat, you may substitute milder chiles; in fact, in other parts of Mexico this is known as Salsa Fresca, Cruda or Mexicana when prepared with jalapeño or serrano chiles. When I want a milder version, I prefer to keep with the habaneros and just decrease the amount so that I can still take pleasure in the unique flavor that goes so well with this style of cooking. Remember, it is easier to add chile heat than to take it away, so start easy. To give this salsa authentic taste, sour oranges are called for; however, the alternatives are very good and considering the relative scarceness of the oranges outside of Mexico and Central America, substitution may be the only option.

Makes about 2 cups

1. Combine all ingredients except cilantro and oil and let sit for 30 to 60 minutes, taste and make adjustments as needed.

2. Add the cilantro and then the oil.

3. Serve at room temperature or slightly chilled.

NOTE: *This is a fresh salsa and tastes best that way. The tomato begins to break down from the acids and although it may taste fine after a few hours or overnight, it is at peak flavor during the first two hours.*

Green Tomatillo Sauce

Water to cook the tomatillos

1 teaspoon salt

2/3 pound tomatillos, husked and
   rinsed

2 to 3 fresh jalapeño or serrano
   chiles OR 2 hot green New
   Mexican chiles OR 1 habanero
   chile, stemmed and seeded

1 medium white onion, roughly
   chopped

3 cloves garlic, toasted and peeled

1/8 cup chopped cilantro leaves

MORE MEXICAN THAN MAYA, this salsa is still very important throughout the Maya lands. It is simple and straightforward and may be used with enchiladas, chilaquiles, tacos, tamales or simply as a table salsa or dip. The amount of chile heat is controlled by the varieties and quantities of chiles used. This sauce tends to thicken with time; add water to restore its original consistency.

Makes about 2 1/2 cups

1. Place enough water to cover the tomatillos in a pot or saucepan and bring to a boil.

2. Add the salt and the tomatillos and cook for 10 minutes, then drain.

3. Place everything in a blender and puree until smooth.

NOTE: *If the salsa is a little too tart, mix in about 1/2 teaspoon of sugar.*

Salsa Verde con Aguacate
Avocado Salsa

SIMILAR TO SALSA VERDE, but hotter and with the addition of avocado, this salsa is great for tacos, salbutes, panuchos, garnachas and many other antojitos. The avocado lends a rich creaminess that helps to balance the extra chile heat.

Makes about 2 cups

1. Place the tomatillos in a pan of boiling, salted water and cook for 5 minutes. Add the onion and garlic cloves and cook for 5 more minutes.

2. Drain and place in a blender with the rest of the ingredients and blend smooth, adding water as needed to allow the blades to run freely.

3 to 4 small tomatillos (about 1/2 cup), husked and rinsed

1 small white onion, peeled and coarsely chopped

3 cloves garlic, peeled

1 habanero chile (or other hot green chiles as you like), charred, stemmed and seeded

2 medium avocados, peeled and pitted

1/8 cup chopped cilantro leaves (optional)

Salt, to taste

Chiltomate
Charred Chile and Tomato Sauce

About 12 ounces ripe tomatoes

1 chile habanero, serrano, New Mexican green or jalapeño

1 small white onion, peeled and thickly sliced (optional)

2 cloves garlic (optional)

3 to 4 epazote leaves OR 1/8 cup cilantro leaves, chopped

1/3 cup sour orange juice OR 1/4 cup sweet orange juice + 2 tablespoons mild vinegar

1/2 teaspoon salt

THIS SALSA FORMS the basis of many recipes throughout the region. It is a simple blend of tomatoes and chiles. There are many variations; the most traditional uses only the molcajete to puree everything, but in modern times the blender has been utilized; most cooks do roast the ingredients, but some boil everything; some versions are strained, most leave it a little chunky; some use onions and garlic while others use only tomatoes and chiles; and finally, some cooks fry the salsa after it is assembled to intensify and sweeten the flavor and others use it as is. Feel free to exercise your own judgment or just follow the directions in the recipe that calls for the chiltomate. The most common chile for this salsa is the habanero; however, in Chiapas, Tabasco, Guatemala and Belize, you will often see a different fresh green chile utilized and the results can be a little milder, again, your choice. Although, as earlier stated, this is usually intended to be part of another recipe, I like to use it as a table salsa when made with cilantro. The rich, complex flavors and the brightness of the chiles and cilantro are a great accompaniment to grilled or smoked meats and seafood, on tacos, chiles rellenos and tamales or just for dipping chips.

Makes about 2 cups

1. Grill the tomatoes, chile, onion and garlic (if using) on a comal or heavy skillet until slightly blackened.

2. Stem and seed the chile, peel the garlic and chop the onion.

3. Coarsely mash the tomatoes, chile, onion and garlic in a molcajete (tamul), mortar and pestle or pulse in a food processor or blender.

4. Mix in the epazote or cilantro, orange juice and salt.

Salsa Esmeralda
Green Salsa with Pumpkinseeds

I CREATED THIS UNIQUE SALSA in Ocosingo, Chiapas, at the Casa Esmeralda, a guesthouse in the central part of the state near the Maya ruins of Tonina. While there I helped the staff prepare a special meal for the guests and we also invited many of the local townspeople. This formulation, inspired by my trip to the *Tianguis* (indigenous market), was so popular that they included it in their repertoire as a signature dish. The bright fruity heat of the habanero chiles and the smoky sweetness of the charred vegetables are balanced by the earthy richness of the pumpkinseeds, resulting in a full-flavored salsa that is not too spicy for most people. Use it as a dip, on grilled or roasted meats or in tacos.

Makes about 2 1/2 cups

1. After the toasted ingredients have cooled, place everything except the pumpkinseeds and the oil in a blender and puree well.

2. Add the seed and oil and blend smooth, adding only enough water to free the blades of the blender.

3. Taste and adjust for salt.

4. Serve at room temperature but store in the refrigerator.

1-1/2 pounds tomatillos, husked, rinsed and well charred

1 medium white onion, peeled, sliced in thirds and pan-roasted

8 cloves garlic, roasted, then peeled

1 or 2 habanero chiles, well charred, stemmed and seeded (you may make this with milder chiles like jalapeño, serrano or poblano, if you like)

1 tablespoon lime juice

2 tablespoons orange juice

Leaves from 1 bunch cilantro

1 cup pumpkinseeds, toasted and finely ground

1 tablespoon vegetable oil

Water as needed

Salt as needed

TJah Bi'ik
Fiery Red Chile Salsa

8 to 12 chiles secos Yucatecos

1 medium white onion, quartered and pan-roasted

3 cloves garlic, pan-toasted, then peeled

1-1/2 tablespoons vegetable oil or lard

3 tablespoons sour orange juice OR
2 tablespoons orange juice +
1 tablespoon mild vinegar OR
3 tablespoons lime juice

Salt, to taste

A BASIC HOT RED SALSA that is requisite on many Maya tables. Use it for tortillas, tacos, eggs or anything that needs a little pick up of heat and flavor. The frying together of the ingredients combines the flavors and adds richness, but be careful to ventilate your kitchen as the odors created can cause you to sneeze, cough and cry. This recipe calls for the small dried chiles of the Yucatán, called Chile Seco; however, you may improvise with a wide variety of dried red chiles as available or according to your taste, such as chiltepe, pico de pájaro, chipotle seco, morita, cascabel, New Mexican caribe, etc. You may also make a green (Yax) version of this using several fresh hot green chiles that have been charred. For a liquid salsa, merely puree in a blender and add a little mild vinegar or water as needed.

Makes about 1-1/4 cups

1. Finely mash the chiles in a molcajete or grind them in a spice grinder or blender.

2. Peel the onion and finely dice; then mince the garlic.

3. Place the oil in a preheated pan and sauté the onion for a minute or two. Add the garlic and chiles and cook for 2 minutes more.

4. Mix in the juice and adjust for salt.

Naranja Ik
Orange-Pumpkinseed Relish

THIS IS MY CONTEMPORARY TAKE on a traditional Yucateca salsa. The original uses ground pumpkinseeds and the juice from sour oranges and is delicious; however, I have substituted diced sweet oranges or tangerines and left the seeds whole for more of a salad or relish.

Makes about 3 cups

1. Peel the oranges with a knife, section and dice.

2. Combine the onion, orange, chiles, lime juice, vinegar and salt; toss and let sit for a few minutes to develop the flavors.

3. Add the seeds, cilantro and oil and gently toss.

4. Serve slightly chilled.

3 medium oranges or tangerines

1 medium red onion, peeled, diced and rinsed (see page 19)

2 tablespoons small, hot red chiles (see Tsah Bí ik recipe, opposite, for suggestions), toasted, stemmed and chopped finely

2 tablespoons lime juice

1 tablespoon mild vinegar

Salt, to taste

1/3 cup green pumpkinseeds, toasted

2 tablespoons chopped cilantro leaves

1 tablespoon olive or vegetable oil

Salsa de Ajo
Garlic Salsa

THIS IS A CAMPECHANA VARIATION on Chile Tamulado that is not quite so palate numbing due to fewer chiles and much more of the sweet, roasted garlic. Use it in the same way as you would its fierce cousin; it is particularly tasty with seafood.

Makes about 3/4 cup

1. Smash all of the ingredients together in a molcajete or mortar and pestle, adding the juice as needed to make a semi-smooth paste.

2 to 3 habanero chiles or other hot green chiles, well-charred and stemmed

12 to 16 cloves garlic, pan-roasted and skinned

2 (1/4-inch-thick) round slices of white onion, pan-roasted and diced fine (optional)

1/2 teaspoon toasted Mexican oregano (optional)

2 to 3 tablespoons sour orange juice or a mix of lime juice and vinegar

Generous dash salt

Salpicón de Rábanos
Radish Salsa

3 tablespoons sour orange juice OR
  2 tablespoons lime juice +
  1 tablespoon sweet orange juice

1 habanero OR 1 to 2 serrano or
  jalapeño chiles, stemmed, seeded
  and minced

Salt, to taste

1 bunch (10 to 12) radishes washed,
  trimmed, cut in half and then
  sliced thin

1 medium red onion, peeled, sliced
  into thin strips and rinsed (see
  page 19)

1/4 cup chopped cilantro leaves
  (NOTE: Substitute mint leaves
  or a combination for an interesting alternative flavor)

1 teaspoon vegetable oil (optional)

THIS SALSA COULD WELL BE described as a salad or relish as it is more of a food accompaniment rather than a dip. *Salpicón* is a Spanish word derived from French that means cut or shredded in little pieces. It functions as a garnish for many Maya plates and the crunchy texture and peppery citrus flavor are an especially good contrast to some of the richer dishes like stews and tamales. Salpicón de Rábanos is also great in tacos.

Makes 1-1/2 cups

1. Combine the juice with the chiles and the salt and let sit for 10 to 15 minutes to tone down the chiles.

2. Mix everything together and serve slightly chilled.

Chile Tumulado (Kut)
Charred Habanero Salsa

THIS ONE IS FOR ALL OF YOU chile heads that appreciate a flavorful sauce that will also make you sweat. Served at domestic tables and in restaurants in most of the Maya lands, it goes by several names: *Kut*, which means crushed or smashed; *tumulado*, which refers to the tamul or molcajete that it is crushed in, or just simply *chilito*. By any name, it is a mind-searing, nonetheless satisfying condiment. Use it anywhere you require extra heat; Chile Tumulado is especially good with seafood and many appetizers or antojitos. Serve it on the side and warn your guests so that they can make an informed decision.

Makes about 3/4 cup

I. Smash all of the ingredients together in a molcajete or mortar and pestle, adding the juice as needed to make a semi-smooth paste.

NOTE: *The optional addition of onion and/or some chopped, charred tomato can help tone down the heat in this salsa.*

4 to 6 habanero chiles (green if you can find them), well-charred and stemmed

4 cloves garlic, pan-roasted and skinned

2 (1/4-inch-thick) round slices of white onion, pan-roasted and diced fine (optional)

2 to 3 tablespoons sour orange juice or a mix of lime juice and mild vinegar

Generous dash salt

Appetizers

Antojitos, or "Little Whims," are one of the mainstays of Mexican food culture. In the towns and cities of the contemporary Maya society, the practice of consuming small-portioned, savory snacks is evident everywhere, although the dishes themselves exhibit the distinctive flavor of the region. Whether consumed as a light meal, part of a formal meal or as a portable, "fast food" street snack, antojitos are part of the daily urban routine.

Many antojitos are made in part with corn; one of the three pillars of pre-Hispanic, Mesoamerican food and a remaining vital component of the campesino modern-day diet.

Corn, whether in tamales, tortillas or other masa-based creations, is used to encase another ingredient or two. Its earthy flavor goes well with savory-spicy flavors and is relatively inexpensive—a perfect snack food. There are as many variations to these antojitos as there are cooks so you should feel free to improvise. Creative uses of leftover meats and salsas/sauces are a good place to start.

These antojitos/appetizers can be served along with cocktails and other beverages, as a starter to other main dishes, combined with other dishes to make up a meal of small plates or just as a tasty snack or light supper dish.

Fried Masa Cups with Picadillo

For the Masa

1-1/4 cups masa harina

1/4 teaspoon salt

*1-1/2 tablespoons pork lard
(optional)*

1 cup very warm water

For the Picadillo

*1/2 the recipe for picadillo from the
Queso Relleno recipe (see page
128) prepared using ground pork
or beef*

OR

*1-1/4 pounds well-seasoned,
browned and drained ground
beef or pork*

Oil for frying

*1 cup shredded cheese for topping
(queso seco, queso fresca, Cotija,
asadero or whatever you prefer
or have on hand)*

GARNACHAS ARE AMONG THE LOADS of masa-based antojitos found all around Mexico. This one uses the Maya-style picadillo but you can make them with any leftover meats or with just black beans too. Feel free to improvise. This recipe is one that I first tasted in San Cristobal de las Casas, Chiapas, and is similar to the garnachas that are served in neighboring Oaxaca. The masa cups and the picadillo may be made in advance; however, the final cooking should be completed just before serving. My favorite condiment for these is Salpicón de Rábanos (see recipe on page 48) and perhaps a little Chile Tumulado or Chiltomate (see recipes on pages 49 and 44) but any salsa will work fine.

Makes 12 to 16 Garnachas (6 to 8 servings)

1. Mix the masa ingredients well until smooth, wrap and set aside for 15 to 30 minutes.

2. Preheat a comal or griddle. Divide the masa into 6 to 8 equal pieces and round each into a ball.

3. Press between plastic in a tortilla press until 2-1/2 inches in diameter (much thicker than tortillas).

4. Cook on the comal until just beginning to brown, flip and cook another 30 to 45 seconds or until slightly browned. Set aside to cool.

5. Lay each cooled disk of masa on the counter and carefully split it with a sharp knife to form two disks, each with a cooked and an uncooked side.

6. With a spoon, scoop out the raw masa in the center of the uncooked side to form a cup or bowl.

7. Preheat a large, heavy skillet with vegetable oil or lard to a depth of 1/2 inch; 350 to 365 degrees F is the ideal frying temperature.

8. Fill each garnacha with some of the picadillo and place in the skillet. Fry

for 2 to 3 minutes until it is golden brown around the edges (it is okay if some of the hot oil gets in with the meat while the garnacha is frying).

9. Drain on paper towels and top with shredded cheese.

10. Top with Salpicon de Rábanos, other salsa and avocado slices or another favorite garnish.

Panuchos and Salbutes
Corn Tortilla Snacks with Savory Toppings

PANUCHOS AND SALBUTES are the distinctively Yucateca version of the corn masa–based snacks popular all around Mexico called gorditas. Panuchos are freshly made corn tortillas that have puffed, are then stuffed with black beans and then fried. Afterwards, they are topped with shredded turkey, chicken or Cochinita Pibil and garnished with Cebollas Moradas Encurtidas (see recipes on pages 126 and 99), shredded cabbage, avocado, possibly some grated cheese and a favorite salsa. Getting the tortillas to properly puff can be a little tricky; many cooks add a little wheat flour to the masa, making it smoother and more likely to puff up while a few even add a little baking powder to the mix. If you cannot get the tortillas to puff, simply put the bean filling on top or sandwich two tortillas together around the beans and proceed. Salbutes are similar to Panuchos but usually skip the black beans. Below you will find a recipe for Salbutes Negros, a variation where the black beans are incorporated into the masa before the tortilla is cooked.

Makes about 16 Panuchos

1. Prepare the masa for the tortillas and divide it into 16 equal parts (keep it covered with a damp towel to prevent drying).

1 recipe Corn Tortillas (see recipe on page 72), optionally replacing 3 to 4 tablespoons of the masa harina with all-purpose flour

1 cup warm Frijoles Colados Yucatecos (see recipe on page 95)

Oil for frying

2 cups shredded meat from Pavo Asado, Pollo Pibil or Cochinita Pibil (see recipes on pages 155, 148 and 126) or other shredded poultry or pork

Garnishes (see recipe intro)

2. Cook the tortillas as directed, attempting to get them to puff.

3. Make an incision with a sharp knife along about 1/4 of the edge of the tortilla and push the blade in to open up the pocket while taking care not to damage the tortilla.

4. Insert about 1 tablespoon of the beans inside, spread around and close the tortilla.

5. Fry the panuchos in 350-degree F oil until golden brown and crispy around the edges (if you fry them completely crisp, the panuchos will become too brittle).

6. Remove from the oil and drain. Top with about 2 tablespoons of the shredded meat and garnish.

7. Serve immediately.

SALBUTES NEGROS

These Salbutes have the beans in the masa rather than stuffing them in the puffed tortillas. Top the same way as for Panuchos, step 6 above.

1. Prepare the masa as for Panuchos, except use only 1-2/3 cups water and mix the cool beans into the masa.

2. Press and cook the tortillas on a hot comal.

3. Fry the tortillas as in step 5 above.

4. Top with meat and garnishes.

Totopos
Fresh Tortilla Chips

20 to 24 corn tortillas (homemade, cooked-on-the-comal tortillas are best but you may use the store-bought varieties too)

1 to 2 quarts vegetable oil for frying

Juice of 1 lime (optional)

Salt, to taste

IN THE UNITED STATES, we are accustomed to light and crispy corn chips from a bag or the restaurant fryer; however, in Mexico, the chips are chewier and more substantial, having been made from fresh tortillas and undercooked slightly. I have learned to prefer this method for my chips. Make sure that your oil is up to temperature before frying the chips or they will be greasy as well as chewy. Use these as you would any corn chip; for dips, nachos, garnishes or with salsa.

Makes about 1 pound of chips

1. Cut the tortillas into 6 wedges each and spread the chips out for an hour or two to dry (turn them over several times while drying to ensure evenness).

2. Heat the oil to 350 degrees F and fry the chips a few at a time until they are just browning and crisping around the edges. Drain well and continue for all of the chips.

3. While the chips are still hot, sprinkle with the lime juice (if using) and liberally salt.

NOTE: *You may store the chips in a sealed plastic bag after they have completely cooled.*

Guacamole

GUACAMOLE IS MORE MEXICAN than Maya, although you will find it on many Maya tables. The rich creaminess of mashed avocado goes well with Maya foods and I have included a version here that is reflective of the flavors of Maya cooking style. Serve it with appetizers like Codzitos and Panuchos (see recipes on pages 60 and 53), with tacos, as a salad or with Totopos (see recipe opposite), soft tortillas or crispy corn chips.

1. Smash the peeled and pitted avocados in a molcajete, in a bowl with a large spoon or potato masher or with your hands until mostly smooth with a few small chunks remaining. (The molcajete gives the best texture; however, it is harder to clean. I usually use my hands; just do not forget to wash them first.)

2. Add the tomatoes, chiles, onion, roasted garlic paste, cumin and cilantro. Mix well, and then season with salt.

3. Wait 5 to 10 minutes for flavors to develop before serving. Guacamole may be stored for a few hours by tightly covering with plastic wrap and chilling, but it does not do well for extended periods.

4. Serve with lime wedges and crumbly sharp cheese like Cotija for garnish.

3 large or 4 to 5 medium avocados

2 small tomatoes, charred and diced

1 habanero chile, charred, stemmed, seeded and finely diced

1/2 cup Cebollas Moradas Encutidas (see recipe on page 99) or red onion, finely diced and rinsed (see page 19)

2 cloves garlic, pan-roasted, peeled and smashed into a smooth paste

Tiny pinch of toasted and ground cumin (optional)

1/4 cup chopped cilantro leaves

Salt, to taste

Lime wedges for garnish

Pumpkinseed Dip

A RICH AND SATISFYING APPETIZER when served with Totopos (see recipe on page 56), Sikil-Pak embodies some of the basic Maya flavors: pumpkinseeds, tomatoes and chiles. Technically Sikil-Pak is a salsa, but I also use it to garnish grilled meats, in tacos and on top of tamales. You can regulate the heat by your choice of chile.

Makes 2 cups

1. Purée the tomatoes, chile and onion in a blender until smooth.

2. Mix with the ground pumpkinseeds and cilantro and enough water to make a smooth, yet thick paste.

3. Add salt to taste and serve.

NOTE: *Sikil-Pak will keep for a day or two in the refrigerator.*

1 pound ripe tomatoes, well charred

1 habanero chile, 2 to 3 jalapeño or serrano chiles, poblano, New Mexican green, Anaheim, etc., charred, stemmed and seeded

1 medium white or red onion, peeled, quartered and pan-roasted (see page 19)

2 cups pumpkinseeds, toasted and ground fine

1/8 cup chopped cilantro

Water as needed

Salt, to taste

Codzitos
Golden Rolled Tacos

24 thin corn tortillas

1 pound shredded poultry or meat
(optional)

Vegetable oil for frying (enough for
a depth of at least 1 inch)

1 cup shredded cheese (queso fresco,
Monterey jack, Cotija, quesa-
dilla, etc.)

Chiltomate (see recipe on page 44)

KNOWN IN OTHER PARTS OF MEXICO as Tacos Dorados or Taquitos, when served in the Yucatán they are filled with flavors that reflect the cooking of the region. *Codz* is a Maya word for rolled up, hence the name. Usually filled with shredded meats and poultry, often leftovers, sometimes they are merely rolled without any filling, fried crisp then served with warm Chiltomate and topped with cheese, then garnished with sliced avocado or Guacamole (see recipe on page 57). Some suggested fillings are Cochinita or Pollo Pibil, Pavo Asado or en Escabeche, Lechón Horneado (see recipes on pages 126, 148, 155, 156 and 137), or simple roast chicken, turkey, pork or beef.

Makes 24

1. Heat the tortillas 1 at a time on a comal or hot griddle to make them pliable.

2. Fill with shredded meat (if using), roll tightly in little cylinders and set aside under a barely damp cloth while completing the others. (You may want to secure each Codzito with a toothpick to keep it from unrolling while cooking. Do not forget to remove the toothpicks before serving.)

3. Fry, a few at a time, in 350- to 365-degree-F oil until golden brown and crispy, drain.

4. Top with the cheese and serve with warm Chiltomate or other chile sauce.

 *Papadzules*

Double-Sauced Enchiladas Filled with Eggs

OFFERED AS AN APPETIZER on restaurant menus around the Yucatán, this preparation is also served at supper or breakfast in many Maya homes. Cleverly utilizing some of the basic staples and seasonings from the past, Papadzules are made with two contrasting sauces; herb-infused pumpkin-seed sauce and the tomato-chile sauce called Chiltomate. The name in Maya means "Food for the Lords," and they were purportedly offered to the first Spanish visitors to the Peninsula. You could also add cooked and shredded chicken or turkey in place of the eggs for a heartier version.

Serves 8

1. Boil the epazote in the salted water for 5 minutes.

2. Mix the toasted and ground pumpkinseeds thoroughly with 3/4 cup of the hot epazote water to form a paste and knead it by hand until some of the greenish-colored oil is released. Carefully collect some of the oil and reserve it for garnish. NOTE: Not all varieties of pumpkinseeds yield the oil in sufficient quantities to use for a garnish. Do not worry; the sauce will still taste good.

3. Blend the pumpkinseed paste with the epazote and enough of the remaining water to obtain a sauce with the consistency of thick gravy. Keep warm.

4. Blend the Chiltomate, then fry in the hot lard or oil until it thickens slightly, 2 to 3 minutes. Season and add enough water to create a thin sauce consistency. Keep warm.

5. Heat the tortillas on a comal or griddle until soft and pliable. Dip the hot tortillas into the pumpkinseed sauce, place some of the hard-boiled eggs into each one and roll up or fold in squares and set side by side on a serving platter. Pour over the remaining pumpkinseed sauce and finally the Chiltomate sauce.

6. Garnish with the toasted pumpkinseeds and drops of the reserved pumpkinseed oil. Papadzules are often also garnished with Cebollas Moradas Encurtidas (see recipe on page 99).

1 or 2 sprigs fresh epazote or 2 tablespoons dried (cilantro may be substituted or added to intensify the flavor and the green color. Do not boil the cilantro; rather, add it in step 3 after the seeds have been kneaded)

2 cups lightly salted water

Water as needed

16 ounces pumpkinseeds, lightly toasted and finely ground (NOTE: you may want to toast a few ounces extra to be left whole for garnish)

1 batch Chiltomate (see recipe on page 44)

1 tablespoon lard or vegetable oil

Salt and pepper, to taste

24 thin white corn tortillas

8 to 10 large hard-boiled eggs, peeled and chopped

Longaniza Asada
Grilled Sausages

LONGANIZA, USUALLY THIN, CHORIZO-LIKE SAUSAGES, are found on menus and in the markets of most Maya communities. Additionally, many families make them from the trim and variety meats from the pig when it is butchered. Simply grilled and served with Chiltomate, roasted red onions and fresh tortillas, they make a tasty appetizer or taco supper along with Frijoles Colados Yucatecos (see recipe on page 95). Variations abound and I have included a recipe for ambitious cooks; however, any firm chorizo or smoked sausage will work or if you are lucky enough to live near a Latin American market, you may purchase some authentic Longaniza.

Serves 6 to 8 as an appetizer and 4 for supper

1. Pan or oven-roast the onion until it is just beginning to soften and the skin has blackened somewhat. Cool.

2. Preheat your char grill.

3. Peel and cut the onions into 1/2-inch squares. Toss the onion squares with the juice, allspice and cilantro. Season to taste and set aside.

4. Grill the Longaniza slowly until nicely browned and releasing its fat. Remove from the grill and let sit a few minutes before serving.

5. Serve whole or in slices along with the onion squares.

LONGANIZA

1. Dissolve the recados in the vinegar.

2. Mix well with the meat, lard and salt, then stuff into the sausage casings.

3. Tie into links about 6 to 8 inches long.

4. Refrigerate, uncovered, overnight to cure.

5. Grill, oven-roast or pan-braise to cook.

---

1 large or 2 small to medium red onions

3 tablespoons sour orange juice OR 1 tablespoon sweet orange juice, 1 tablespoon lime juice and 1 tablespoon fruity, mild vinegar

1/2 teaspoon toasted and ground allspice

1 tablespoon chopped cilantro (optional)

Salt and pepper, to taste

1-1/2 pounds Longaniza (recipe follows), firm chorizo or smoked sausages

1 tablespoon Recado Negro (see recipe on page 30) OR 1 tablespoon Recado de Escabeche (see recipe on page 32) + 1 tablespoon mild chile powder, toasted

1 tablespoon Recado Colorado (see recipe on page 29)

1-1/2 tablespoons mild, fruity vinegar

1-1/2 pounds ground pork

1/3 cup lard, softened but not melted

1-1/2 teaspoons salt

Sausage casings

Tortitas de Frijol
Bean-Filled Masa Fritters

1 pound baby lima beans, small
white beans, butter beans or
black-eyed peas

1 sprig fresh epazote or 1 tablespoon
dried

1/2 cup pumpkinseeds, toasted and
finely ground

1/4 cup chopped cilantro leaves
(you may substitute mint or
fresh oregano here)

3/4 cup green onions or scallions,
finely chopped

1 tablespoon mild vinegar

Salt and black pepper, to taste

1 recipe masa for Corn Tortillas (see
recipe on page 72)

Vegetable oil for frying

THESE SIMPLE AND TASTY LITTLE BOTANAS are also known as *polcanes*; Maya for snake heads. They are usually made with fresh ibes, a seasonal treat, similar to baby lima beans. Traditionally, the tortitas are wrapped in Yerba Santa (root beer plant) or banana leaves and baked in the Pibil or steamed, although these days polcanes are more often fried in oil until crispy. Either way, they are great when served with a little salsa alongside.

Makes 16 to 18

1. Cook the beans with the epazote until tender, drain and mix with the pumpkinseeds; cool.

2. Mix in the cilantro, green onions and vinegar and season with salt and pepper.

3. Divide the masa into 16 to 18 equal portions and press out each portion of masa as directed in the tortilla recipe, peeling off the top sheet of plastic while holding the tortilla in your hand.

4. Place a spoonful of the bean and pumpkinseed mixture in the center of each tortilla and fold the masa around to enclose. Shape into a ball, oval sphere or a flat patty and set aside under a damp towel while preparing the rest.

5. Fry in 350-degree-F oil until golden brown. Drain and serve hot.

NOTE: *To prepare the more traditional version, before cooking, wrap each Polcane Tortita in Yerba Santa or pre-toasted banana leaves, secure and steam for 35 minutes or bake at 350 degrees F for 45 minutes. To serve, leave the Yerba Santa leaves on but unwrap if using banana leaves.*

Botanas de Papas
Cantina Potatoes

CANTINAS IN MEXICO TRADITIONALLY serve complimentary botanas, tapas-like small plates of food, along with the beverages. I enjoyed this potato salad at Eladio's, a well-known Merida establishment with white-clad waiters scurrying about bearing trays of frosty cervezas and marvelous Yucateco food on a hot and muggy afternoon.

Serves 6 as an appetizer or side dish

1. Gently mix everything except the oil, season with salt and pepper and let sit a few minutes for the flavors to blend.

2. Stir in the oil.

NOTE: *This recipe tastes even better when stored for a few hours or overnight.*

1-1/2 pounds potatoes, cooked, peeled and cut into bite-sized pieces (waxy varieties like red or white rose or Yukon gold work well)

1/2 cup Cebollas Mordadas Encurtidas (see recipe on page 99) OR raw red onion, rinsed (see page 19) and diced

1 sweet bell pepper or 2 mild green chiles, charred, peeled, seeded and diced

2 tablespoons sour orange juice or lime juice

1 tablespoon fruity, mild vinegar

1 tablespoon fresh oregano OR 2 tablespoons fresh cilantro, chopped

Salt and pepper, to taste

1-1/2 tablespoons olive oil

Plátanos Rellenos
Stuffed Plantains

4 large plantains, ripened yellow but without very much blackening

1/2 pound ground beef

1/2 pound ground pork

1 sprig fresh epazote or 2 teaspoons dried

2 cloves garlic, peeled and finely chopped

Vegetable oil for frying

1 medium white onion, peeled and finely chopped

1 sweet red, yellow or green pepper, finely chopped

1 medium tomato, diced small

1 teaspoon Recado Colorado (see recipe on page 29) or 1 teaspoon achiote paste

1/2 teaspoon ground canela (cinnamon)

1/2 teaspoon ground allspice

Pinch of ground cloves

1/4 cup raisins

1/4 cup green olives, chopped

POPULAR ALL ALONG THE GULF COAST, this recipe for Plátanos Rellenos comes from tropical Tabasco where plantains are always in good supply. While plantains are in the banana family, they are more like a potato because of their starchy quality. Here, they are filled with a type of picadillo, but they can be easily stuffed with almost any tasty filling: black beans, shredded poultry, cheese, fruits, etc. Serve as an early course at comida, along with eggs at breakfast or brunch or as an evening snack.

Makes about 18

1. Cut the ends off the plantains, then cut in half (leave the peel on). Cook in boiling salted water for 20 to 25 minutes until the flesh of the plantain is soft. Drain and set aside to cool.

2. Cook the meat, along with the epazote and garlic cloves, in enough salted water to cover. Drain.

3. Heat the oil in a heavy skillet, add the onion and peppers and sauté for 2 minutes.

4. Add the tomatoes, cook for 1 minute more, then add the meat, canela, Recado Colorado, allspice and cloves. Cook while stirring until heated thoroughly. Add in the raisins, olives and almonds and mix well. Remove from the heat and season with salt and pepper.

5. Remove the peels and mash the plantains (a potato ricer or food mill works well for this).

6. Using 2 sheets of heavy plastic, form 3-inch-diameter "tortillas" with the mashed plantains either with a tortilla press or by hand.

7. Place a spoonful of the picadillo in the center of a tortilla and fold the plantain around the filling to form a cylinder that fully encases the picadillo.

NOTE: *It helps to keep your hands wet while handling the mashed plantain; it prevents sticking.*

8. Fry in 350- to 365-degree F oil until golden brown. Drain.

Serve with Salsa Verde, Salsa Verde con Aguacate, Chiltomate (see recipes on pages 42, 43 and 44) or other favorite sauce along with some sour cream.

1/4 cup toasted, sliced almonds (optional)

Salt and pepper, to taste

2 tablespoons vegetable oil or lard

Niños Envueltos

Meat- and Rice-Stuffed Leaves

12 large Swiss chard or beet green leaves, blanched and quickly chilled, stems removed and cut in half

1/2 the recipe for Picadillo from the Queso Relleno recipe (see page 128) prepared using ground pork or beef or a mixture of the two

1-1/2 cups cooked rice

2 tablespoons masa harina or bread crumbs

1 egg, beaten

1 batch Chiltomate (see recipe on page 44)

NIÑOS ENVUELTOS HAS MANY incarnations throughout Latin America, but they all involve leaves that are stuffed with meat or vegetable mixtures. This recipe uses the Yucatán-style Picadillo mixed with rice. Although the original version is wrapped in chaya leaves, a healthy spinach-like plant consumed all over southern Mexico, I have substituted chard, which is easier to find and a little more durable. I have also used Yerba Santa successfully as an interestingly flavored variation. Regularly served as an appetizer, these little packages also make for a nice main course.

Serves 6 to 8 as appetizers and 4 for a main course

1. Pat the chard leaves dry and lay out on the counter with the pale side facing up.

2. Mix the Picadillo, rice and masa harina together with the egg and divide between the leaves.

3. Wrap each leaf carefully around the filling to make a sealed packet. Chill for at least a few minutes to firm.

4. Heat the Chiltomate in a pan, gently place the packets in the sauce, cover and simmer for 12 to 15 minutes to heat through.

5. Serve with the sauce.

Corn and Bread Dishes

CORN

CORN IS THE FOUNDATION of Mexican cooking, and in the Maya world, it is no different. The corn plant was sacred to the ancient Maya and was one of the deities most revered. Corn for masa is treated with the mineral lime (not the fruit) or calcium oxide, called Cal in Spanish. Originally, the indigenous people of the Americas used ashes from wood fires to treat the corn. This process causes the corn kernel to shed its outer skin and swell up. A similar process is used to produce hominy. Untreated corn is not very digestible by humans; however, when treated with an alkali, such as ashes or lime, over 90 percent of the nutrients become usable. The result is known as *nixtamal* in Nahuatl or *sakan* in Maya. Treated corn combined with beans provides a complete array of essential amino acids and protein and is able to sustain human life. This combination was the basis of the indigenous diet on the continent and continues to be an integral part of modern-day Mexican/Maya cooking.

Corn Tortillas

2 cups dry masa harina

1/2 teaspoon salt

1-7/8 cups (approximately) warm water (95 to 115 degrees F)

THERE IS NOTHING TO COMPARE to the taste and texture of a corn tortilla fresh off the comal or griddle. I was at first intimidated by the process but finally gave it a try. I found that after a few mishaps and a little practice, it became almost second nature to me. I now make them at home frequently.

Makes 16 to 20 three-and-a-half-inch tortillas

1. Place the dry ingredients in a mixing bowl and slowly add the water while stirring with a fork until the dough comes together into a ball. Knead the dough several times by hand until smooth. Wrap in plastic and let stand for at least 15 minutes.

2. Preheat a comal, heavy skillet or griddle to medium-high heat (350 degrees F).

3. Form some masa into a 1-inch-diameter ball, adding a few drops of cool water to moisten if needed. Place the ball between 2 sheets of plastic (a freezer bag split into 2 sheets works well) and flatten in a tortilla press or by hand to about 1/16 inch thick.

4. Peel off the top sheet of plastic and gently transfer the tortilla from the other sheet to your bare palm, invert it over the comal or griddle and gently slide it onto the cooking surface. Cook for about 20 to 30 seconds and turn over. Cook for 30 to 45 seconds more and flip over again. Gently pushing down with a spatula should cause the tortilla to puff slightly (an important criteria for good Mexican tortillas). Properly cooked tortillas will have light brown speckles while remaining pliable.

5. Keep the cooked tortillas in a kitchen towel, tortilla warmer or cloth napkin to keep warm while cooking others and for serving. Serve immediately.

▨ Tamales

Perhaps among the first of many portable foods in Mesoamerica, tamales have become the food of celebration all around Mexico. Too rich for daily consumption, tamales today represent the hearth rite of Mexican kitchens and are reserved for special occasions: weddings, feast days, religious holidays, funerals and Day of the Dead celebrations. The name is derived from the Aztec *tamalli*; however, archeologists have found that the Maya were preparing tamales long before the Aztecs dominated central Mexico. Tamales were originally formed simply from treated and ground corn, *nixtamal* or *sakal*, wrapped around a filling of vegetables, seeds, eggs, meat from wild game or seafood, often seasoned with spices and chiles. Then the Spanish introduced the domestic pig, and the rich lard that was produced from that animal contributes flavor, richness, some leavening and improved texture to the tamales. Generally, in Maya cooking, like in most of Mexico, banana leaves and dried cornhusks are the wrapping materials, although some other specialty plant leaves are used in regional versions. Either type of wrapping may substitute for the other, although each kind lends its own subtle flavor to the finished product.

Many tamale recipes are derived from various meats prepared for other main meals—leftovers. Once you master the several variations of the masa, you will be able to create your own recipes with meats, vegetables and seafood.

Masa for Tamales

In Maya regions, freshly ground masa is usually used when tamales are prepared. Outside of that area, it can sometimes be difficult to obtain, hence I have included a method for duplicating that masa by using masa harina, dried flour made from the treated corn and generally available throughout the United States and in parts of Canada and Europe as well. Although some purists may disagree, I have found that better-than-acceptable results from using this masa harina substitute for the *nixtamal* allow me to produce tamales that would normally require many more hours of soaking and hand grinding of corn. If you live near a tortillerilla, you may purchase fresh masa there, but be sure that it does not already have the lard (manteca) added. Also, in some supermarkets in the southwest and in cities that have a large Hispanic population, you can purchase fresh masa. All of the recipes that follow work equally well with either method.

Fresh Masa Substitute

Makes about 2 pounds

3-2/3 cups masa harina

2 cups hot water

1. Mix well by hand for about 5 minutes until smooth.

2. Cover with plastic wrap and let sit for at least 30 minutes before using.

Tamal de Frijol Tierno
Black Bean Tamales

3/4 pound pork lard or shortening

2 pounds fresh masa or Masa Substitute (see recipe on page 73)

1-1/2 teaspoons salt

1 recipe Frijoles Negros de Olla (see recipe on page 94), drained in a coarse strainer

30 Yerba Santa leaves OR 2 teaspoons lightly toasted and ground aniseed

30 dried cornhusks, soaked until pliable and wiped dry

THESE TAMALES FROM THE INDIGENOUS Maya villages in the highlands of Chiapas have no filling. They have black beans mixed in with the masa and are scented with the anisey flavored leaves of Yerba Buena or *Momón*, as it is called there. I once tried making them with ground aniseed added to the masa, since Yerba Santa is hard to come by where I live, and I was very satisfied with the results. Serve these tamales with a little Chiltomate, Salsa Esmeralda (see recipes on pages 44 and 45) or other salsa, or simply as a side to many meat dishes.

Makes about 30 tamales

1. Whip the lard in a mixer or by hand until fluffy.

2. Add the masa bit by bit while continuing to whip until 2/3 of the masa is incorporated.

3. Add the salt (and the aniseed, if using) and start adding the beans alternately with the rest of the masa until it is all mixed together.

4. Lay out the cornhusks, place a Yerba Santa leaf inside (if using), and spread about 4 rounded tablespoons of the masa over each leaf.

5. Roll up each cornhusk and fold the end or use strips of husk tied to secure.

6. Steam for about 1-1/4 hours.

7. Let rest for 15 to 20 minutes before serving to firm up the masa.

Tamalitos de X'Pelon
Tamales with Black-Eyed Peas

X'PELON, OR ESPELON, is a type of bean similar to the black-eyed pea. These beans are added whole to the masa in this recipe, and the tamale is filled with both chicken and pork, moistened with "gravy" called *Kol*, which is made from the masa and the cooking liquid. You may use either chicken, pork or both, and it may be cooked especially for the recipe or use a leftover meat.

Makes about 30 tamales

1. For the filling, cook the chicken and the pork together with the remaining filling ingredients, seasonings, and water to cover until the pork is tender. Remove the meat and shred. Strain and reserve 1-1/2 cups of the broth.

2. To make the Kol, sauté the onion in the lard or vegetable oil until slightly browned, add the tomato, epazote and 3/4 cup of the broth. Bring to a boil and mix in the masa until smooth. Add the shredded meat and remove from the heat.

3. For the tamale masa, whip the lard in a standup mixer or in a bowl by hand until fluffy. Add the masa a little at a time and continue whipping. When half of the masa is mixed in, start adding 3/4 cup broth, salt and the remaining masa alternately until all is incorporated and fluffy. Fold in the beans.

(continued on page 77)

For the Filling

1 pound chicken pieces

1 pound pork shoulder or loin, cut into 2-inch cubes

2 tablespoons Recado Colorado (see recipe on page 29)

Water to cover

1/2 cup roughly chopped onion

4 cloves garlic, smashed and peeled

1 sprig epazote OR 1 tablespoon dried

1 sprig fresh oregano OR 1 tablespoon Mexican oregano, toasted

1/2 teaspoon cumin, toasted

1 teaspoon salt

For the Tamale Masa

3/4 pound pork lard or vegetable shortening

2 pounds fresh masa or Masa Substitute (see recipe on page 73), 1/4 cup reserved for the Kol

3/4 cup strained broth from cooking the meat, chicken broth or water

1-1/2 teaspoons salt

1-1/2 cups cooked X'pelon or black-eyed peas

4. Spread the masa on each banana leaf to make a 4x4-inch square 1/2 inch thick. Divide the meat between the tamales and fold to make a sealed package. Secure by tying strips of banana leaf or string.

5. Steam for 1-1/2 hours and allow to cool for 15 to 20 minutes before serving with your favorite sauce or salsa.

For the Kol

1/2 cup onion, diced

2 teaspoons lard or vegetable oil

1/2 cup chopped tomato

1 tablespoon epazote, chopped

3/4 cup strained cooking broth from the meat OR chicken broth with 1 teaspoon Recado Colorado (see recipe on page 29)

1/4 cup reserved masa

30 banana leaf rectangles, plus extra for tying, toasted to make pliable

Tamalitos Chayas
Little Tamales with Greens

For the Filling

2 pounds ground pork

3 bay leaves

2 sprigs epazote OR 2 sprigs
   oregano and 2 sprigs fresh thyme
   OR 2 tablespoons toasted
   Mexican oregano

1 medium white onion, cut in half

1 tablespoon lard or vegetable oil

1-1/2 pounds ripe tomatoes,
   charred, then pureed with 1/2 of
   the white onion and strained

1 cup pitted green olives, chopped

2 tablespoons capers

2/3 cup raisins

1 sweet red pepper or green pepper,
   seeded and diced

1 hot yellow, jalapeño or serrano
   chile, seeded and finely minced

1 teaspoon whole allspice, toasted
   and ground

Salt and pepper, to taste

CHAYA (*CNIDOSCOLU CHAYAMANSA*) IS A PLANT native to tropical America with a spinach-like flavor. Although the flavor of spinach is similar, more durable greens often make a better substitute. I first tasted these little tamales in a vegetarian coffee house in Palenque, Chiapas, a small town outside of the spectacular Mayan ruins of the same name. At one time this was one of the more important cradles of Mesoamerican ancient civilization where the Olmec culture preceded the Mayans. In the area you can witness the mixing of the indigenous styles of mountainous Chiapas with the lowland and Gulf Coast cooking of Tabasco and the Yucatán. This version contains pork, but you can easily make a vegetarian version using the instructions in the recipe. These Tamalitos are similar to *Dzotobichay*, a Yucatán tamale also made with chaya leaves but filled with pumpkinseeds and hard-boiled eggs, another vegetarian option. Serve with Chiltomate (see recipe on page 44).

Makes 32 to 36 tamales

1. Place the pork in a pan with 2 cups of water along with the herbs and 1/2 of the onion until it is cooked, approximately 20 minutes. Drain and remove the herbs and onion.

2. Heat the lard or oil and fry the pureed tomato and onion. After 1 minute add the remaining ingredients including the meat. Simmer over a low flame until the mixture has thickened. Salt and pepper, to taste.

Tamalitos

1. Cook the chaya (or other) leaves in 2 quarts of boiling, lightly salted water until they are tender, taking care that they do not become too soft. Drain and reserve the water.

2. Mix the masa with the cooled water in which the chaya leaves were cooked and strain it using cheesecloth or a fine sieve.

3. Gently heat this in a heavy saucepan or Dutch oven until it comes to a boil, then add the lard and salt to taste. Cook the mixture, stirring often (a wooden spoon works well for this), for 15 to 20 minutes or until cooked through and smooth. You can tell it is ready when a small amount is pressed on a banana leaf and it pulls away easily and cleanly.

4. Toast the banana leaves over an open flame or on a comal or griddle until the inside of the leaf turns shiny and the leaf is pliable (see page 19).

5. Place some chaya (or alternate) leaves on top of the banana leaf rectangles, add a large tablespoon of cooked masa and spread out about 3 inches by 3 inches. Place 2 tablespoons of the filling on top, cover with another chaya leaf and form the tamales by folding the sides of the leaf in towards the center, then do the same with the ends until a small rectangular package is formed. Use strips of the leaves to secure the bundle if you like. Place it lengthwise in a tamale steamer or plain steamer. Repeat this until you have used up the entire filling, making sure to leave a little space around each of the tamales to allow the air to circulate. Steam for 1-1/4 hours or until the tamales come off the banana leaf easily when they are unwrapped.

Serve the tamales arranged on a platter, with sauce over the top and sprinkle with ground, toasted pumpkinseeds and chopped egg or crumbled cheese.

For the Tamalitos

2 pounds chaya leaves OR spinach, Swiss chard, beet greens or collard greens, stems removed and cut into pieces 2 inches across

2 pounds fresh masa or Masa Substitute (see recipe on page 73)

3/4 pound pork lard OR 1/2 pound shortening and 1/4 pound butter (if making the vegetarian version)

1 teaspoon salt

32 rectangles of banana leaves (plus extra for ties), 10 inches long and 8 inches wide OR 32 cornhusks for tamales, soaked

Tamales de la Boda Colados
Wedding Tamales

For the Masa

3 cups water

2 pounds fresh masa or Masa Substitute (see recipe on page 73), reserve 2/3 cup for the Kol

1-1/2 teaspoons salt

2/3 pound pork lard

For the Kol

2 cups reserved cooking broth from the chicken, strained

2/3 cup reserved masa

48 (8x12-inch) banana leaves, plus extra for ties, toasted to make pliable (see page 19)

For the Filling

3 to 3-1/2 pounds chicken pieces, cooked and shredded in large pieces (Cook the same as in Muc-bil Pollo, see recipe on page 84, without the pork. Reserve 2 cups of the broth for the Kol.)

1 large or 2 small red onions, peeled and thinly sliced

1-1/2 pounds tomatoes, sliced into 24 slices

8 to 10 epazote leaves OR 1/3 cup oregano or cilantro leaves, chopped

THESE TAMALES ARE CUSTOMARILY served at engagement parties and weddings, hence the title. The Colado refers to the straining of the masa through linen or a colander before cooking it and mixing it with the lard. All of this extra effort results in a smooth, custard-like texture in the finished masa inside of the tamales.

Makes about 24 tamales

1. For the masa, mix the water and the masa until smooth. Press through a coarse strainer or cheesecloth and discard what remains. (You may omit the straining if using the masa substitute made with masa harina.)

2. Place in a heavy saucepan with the salt and cook over medium-low heat, stirring constantly until thickened. Add the lard a little at a time. Make sure all of the lard is incorporated before adding more. Lower the heat and continue stirring and cooking until the masa begins to pull away from the pan and is smooth and shiny (12 to 15 minutes).

3. Pour into a 9x13-inch pan and smooth to make it uniformly thick (3/4 to 1 inch). Set aside to cool.

4. Mix the reserved broth and the masa together until smooth for the Kol. Cook on low heat while stirring for 10 to 15 minutes until thickened like gravy.

5. Lay out the banana leaves. Cut the masa into 24 equal squares.

6. For each tamale, place a square of masa on top of the leaf, add a tablespoon of the Kol, some chicken, an onion and a tomato slice and a sprinkle of epazote or alternative herb.

7. Close the tamale by folding each side in to form a package and secure with a tie or string.

8. Steam for 1 to 1-1/4 hours. Turn off the heat and remove the lid. Let rest for 15 to 20 minutes before serving.

Vaporcitos
Basic Steamed Tamales

VAPORCITOS MEANS "LITTLE STEAMED ONES" and these tamales are more "everyday" tamales than many of the other recipes in this book. The fillings may vary from pork, chicken, or a combination of the two, to seafood or vegetarian. For a Caribbean flavor, replace the broth in the masa with coconut milk. While banana leaves are the usual wrapper, soaked cornhusks work equally well. Serve as is, or with some of your favorite salsa alongside. In some areas, a hot chile (habanero, xcatic, jalapeño or serrano) is charred, minced and added to the masa for extra flavor and heat. Feel free to use this basic recipe to create your own favorites. These tamales may be frozen after they are cooked. Place them in a steamer for 15 to 20 minutes to reheat.

Makes about 24 tamales

1. To make the masa, whip the lard in a stand-up mixer or by hand until fluffy. Add the masa incrementally while continuing to whip. When half of the masa is incorporated, add the salt, then continue with the masa, alternating with the 2 cups broth until everything has been added and the masa is smooth and fluffy (a small piece should float in cold water).

2. To make the Kol, mix the reserved broth and 1/2 cup reserved masa together until smooth. Cook on low heat while stirring for 10 to 15 minutes until thickened like gravy. NOTE: No Kol is needed for the Sikil-Pak tamales.

3. For the filling, add the vegetables, if using, to the Kol. Mix with the meat.

4. Toast the banana leaves to make them pliable (see page 19). Spread some masa on each leaf about 1/4 inch thick and 4 inches square. Top with some of the meat and fold the sides of the tamale together to enclose the filling. Then fold the ends to overlap and tie with strips of the leaves or twist the ends and tie them securely for a rounded tamale.

5. Steam for 1-1/4 hours, remove from the heat and uncover. Let sit for 15 to 20 minutes for the masa to firm up.

For the Masa
3/4 pound pork lard or vegetable shortening

2 pounds fresh masa or Masa Substitute (see recipe on page 73), reserve 1/2 cup for the Kol

1-1/2 teaspoons salt

2 cups broth from cooking the meat, chicken broth, coconut milk or water

For the Kol
1-1/2 cups reserved broth from cooking the meat or chicken broth with 1 teaspoon Recado Colorado (see recipe on page 29)

1/2 cup reserved masa

For the Filling
1/2 cup diced tomatoes, 1 diced sweet pepper and 1/2 cup diced onion, sautéed briefly in a little lard or vegetable oil (optional)

3 pounds chicken, pork or a combination, cooked in the manner of Muc-bil Pollo (see recipe on page 84), shredded OR 1 recipe Sikil-Pak (see recipe on page 59)

Banana leaves (cut in 10x7-inch rectangles) or cornhusks (soaked) for 24 tamales (a few extras to make strips to tie the tamales)

Tamalou Tutiwah
Maya Calendar Tamal

3/4 pound pork lard or vegetable shortening

1 teaspoon salt

2 pounds fresh masa or Masa Substitute (see recipe on page 73)

1/4 cup water

1 teaspoon Recado Colorado or Acluòte Paste, dissolved in 1 tablespoon mild vinegar (optional)

2/3 cup pumpkinseeds, well toasted and ground fine

1 cup cooked baby lima beans or small white beans, mashed

1 tablespoon chopped epazote (optional)

Dash salt

2 tablespoons water

2 large or several small banana leaves, toasted to make pliable, plus extra for ties

THIS IS A SINGLE TAMAL that emulates the Maya thirteen-month calendar. Tutiwah was a ceremonial corn bread with thirteen layers of fillings. Although this has only one layer, there are thirteen indentations with additional filling in each. In present-day Yucatán bakeries, they sell *Tutis*, which is an oven-baked, yeasted bread that is usually layered with cheese. This tutiwah makes for a fun appetizer when served with salsa and a slice is also often placed in the bottom of the bowl with Pavo en Relleno Negro.

Makes about 13 servings

1. Whip the lard until fluffy; add the salt, then the masa a little at a time along with the 1/4 cup water and Recado, fusing. Whip until fluffy and a little piece will float in cold water.

2. Reserve 3 tablespoons of the seeds and mix the rest with the beans, epazote, dash of salt and 2 tablespoon water.

3. Lay out the banana leaves shiny side up. Overlap if using more than one. Spread half of the masa on the banana leaves to make a circular disc 1/2 inch thick. Spread the bean-and-seed mixture over the disk and top with the remaining masa.

4. Make 13 indentations with your thumb around the edges of the circle. Divide the remaining ground seeds between these indentations, then carefully close the banana leaves around the filling and secure.

5. Place on a well-oiled baking sheet and place in a 350-degree-F oven on the top shelf. Place a roasting pan with water on the lower shelf under the tamal.

6. Bake for 45 minutes to 1 hour, let rest for 15 to 20 minutes to firm up, cut open and serve.

Muc-bil Pollo
Tamale Pie for Day of the Dead

For the Filling

1 pound pork butt or stew meat cut
in 2-inch pieces

2 quarts water

10 to 12 cloves garlic (1 head), toasted and peeled

1 white onion, cut in half and
toasted with the peel on

1 to 2 habanero chiles, charred and
left whole

2 sprigs fresh epazote OR 1 tablespoon dry

1 tablespoon Mexican oregano,
toasted

2 tablespoons sour orange juice or
mild, fruity vinegar

3 tablespoons Recado Colorado (see
recipe on page 29)

2 teaspoons salt

1/2 teaspoon black pepper

2 pounds chicken pieces, bone in

For the Kol

1 cup reserved masa

2-1/2 cups strained broth from
cooking the meats

IN ALL OF LATIN AMERICA, the Day of the Dead, *Dia de los Muertos,* is an important celebration that spans roughly November 1 to 3. Rather than a sad and gloomy occasion, it is a time for festivity, religious rituals, special foods and fond remembrance of loved ones, a family reunion for both the living and the dearly departed. In Maya lands, this holiday is known as Hanal Pixan, and the customs are as reflective of ancient Maya traditions and beliefs in synergy with Catholic practices.

Probably the most recognized of all the dishes prepared for *Hanal Pixan* in the Yucatán is Muc-bil Pollo. In addition to serving it to family and visitors, a slice is invariably placed on the altar along with favorite beverages, sweets, flowers and copal incense, all to entice the deceased family members' spirits to return for a brief sojourn. More of a tamale pie than a tamale, Muc-bil Pollo is baked after wrapping it in banana leaves and placing it in an earthenware pot. Tradition calls for cooking in the Pibil dug in the ground, although these days it is often carried to the local bakery or baked in the home oven. This dish lends itself well to preparing the filling in advance and when it is in the oven, very little more attention is required; perfect for a time of celebration.

Makes 10 to 12 servings

1. To make the filling, place the pork in the 2 quarts of water and add the garlic, onion, chile, herbs, juice, recado, salt and pepper. Bring to a boil and cook for 30 minutes. Add the chicken and cook at a slow boil, occasionally skimming any foam off the top, until the chicken is done (about 1 hour).

2. Remove the meat from the broth, cool and coarsely shred. Strain the broth; reserve 2-1/2 cups for the Kol and 3/4 cup for the masa. Save 1 chile for the masa.

3. Make the kol by mixing the 1 cup reserved masa with the 2-1/2 cups of broth until smooth. Slowly simmer for about 15 to 20 minutes, until the kol has thickened like gravy, then remove from the heat.

4. For the masa, gently heat the lard to just melt and with a stand-up mixer or by hand, beat it into the masa, alternately with the 3/4 cup broth and the chopped chile and salt until smooth. Fold in the beans, if using.

5. Toast the banana leaves to make them pliable (see page 19), and tear several into strips as ties. Place one leaf in the bottom of a large casserole, Dutch oven or heavy roasting pan, then lay the ties in a cross. On top of the ties, line with enough leaves to come up the side and overlap on top.

6. Place 2/3 of the masa in the bottom and up the sides about 1/2 inch thick. Mix 1/2 of the kol with the meats and place on the masa. Pour the remaining kol over the top, then lay the tomato, pepper and onion slices over the top of that.

7. Top with the remaining masa and pinch together the edges with the bottom to make a sealed package around the filling. Place a banana leaf on top and fold the edges of the other leaves over that. Tie the pieces of the cross to secure the package.

8. Bake at 375 degrees F for 1-1/2 hours. Remove from the oven and allow to sit for 20 to 30 minutes. Cut open the package and carefully open (there will still be some hot steam).

9. Serve family style on the banana leaves or cut into individual portions and garnish with chopped hard-boiled eggs.

For the Masa

3/4 pound pork lard

2 pounds fresh masa or Masa Substitute (see recipe on page 73), reserve 1 cup for the Kol

3/4 cup strained broth from cooking the meats

1 habanero chile from cooking the meats, stemmed, seeded and finely chopped

1-1/2 teaspoons salt

1-1/2 cups cooked black-eyed peas (optional)

Banana leaves for wrapping

2 large tomatoes, sliced

1 sweet bell pepper, seeded and sliced

1 white or red onion, peeled and sliced

Tamalitos de Pescado o Mariscos
Caribbean Fish or Seafood Tamales

For the Masa

3/4 pound pork lard or vegetable shortening

2 pounds fresh masa or Masa Substitute (see recipe on page 73)

1-1/2 teaspoons salt

2 cups coconut milk mixed with 1 teaspoon Recado Colorado (see recipe on page 29), optional

For the Filling

1-1/2 tablespoons Recado Colorado (see recipe on page 29)

1 teaspoon salt

1/2 teaspoon black pepper

4 tablespoons sour orange juice OR 2 tablespoons lime juice and 2 tablespoons sweet orange juice

1/8 cup chopped cilantro (optional)

2-1/2 to 3 pounds fresh fish, shell-fish or other seafood (uncooked), alone or in combination, in bite-sized pieces

Banana leaves (cut in 10x7-inch rectangles) for 24 tamales (plus a few extras to make strips to tie the tamales)

THIS STYLE OF TAMALE IS SEEN along the Caribbean coast of Quintana Roo, Belize and Guatemala and at times along the Gulf Coast in Campeche and Tabasco. They are similar to *vaporcitos* but use coconut milk in the masa instead of meat broth. Any type of fish or seafood will work in these little tamales, alone or in combinations.

Makes 24 tamales

1. To make the masa, whip the lard in a stand-up mixer or by hand until fluffy. Add the masa incrementally while continuing to whip. When half of the masa is incorporated, add the salt, then continue with the masa, alternating with the coconut milk until everything has been added and the masa is smooth and fluffy (a small piece should float in cold water).

2. For the filling, dissolve the recado, salt and pepper in the juices, add the cilantro and then toss with the seafood.

3. Toast the banana leaves to make them pliable (see page 19). Spread some masa on each leaf about 1/4 inch thick and 4 inches square. Top with some of the seafood and fold the sides of the tamale together to enclose the filling. Then fold the ends to overlap and tie with strips of the leaves or twist the ends and tie them securely for a rounded tamale.

4. Steam for 1-1/4 hours, remove from the heat and uncover. Let sit for 15 to 20 minutes for the masa to firm up.

Banana Bread

THIS RECIPE COMES FROM the state of Tabasco, although many versions may be found around the Maya lands. Ripe bananas are the key to the flavor. Using either masa harina or corn meal creates an interesting texture and flavor. Use this as breakfast bread, like a shortcake, topped with fruit and whipped or ice cream for dessert or as an accompaniment to a savory main dish like *Carribean Coconut Fish Soup* (see recipe on page 177) or *Olla Podrida* (see recipe on page 125). You may make this banana bread in a round or square baking dish, a loaf pan or in individual muffin tins. Chopped nuts and/or raisins may also be added to the mix if you like.

Makes about 4 to 6 servings

1. Sift the first 5 ingredients together to mix and set aside.

2. Cream the butter with the sugar and vanilla then add the eggs, one at a time, continuing to beat fluffy.

3. Mix in the bananas and yogurt.

4. Fold this wet mixture into the sifted dry mix and gently stir until just combined. Do not over mix. Fold in the nuts and/or raisins if using.

5. Grease a 9-inch round or square baking pan, loaf pan, or 1 dozen muffin cups and spoon in the batter.

6. Bake in a preheated 350 degree oven 40 minutes for the round or square pan, 55 minutes for the loaf pan or 25 to 30 minutes for muffins, until golden brown.

7. Cool for 10 to 15 minutes and remove from the pan.

1-1/2 cups all-purpose flour

1-1/4 cups coarse masa harina (tamale grind) or enriched corn meal

1/2 teaspoon salt

1-1/2 teaspoons baking powder

1/4 teaspoon baking soda

6 ounces butter (1-1/2 sticks), softened at room temperature

3/4 to 1-1/4 cups sugar (depending on how sweet you want the bread)

2 teaspoons vanilla extract, optional

2 eggs

2 medium-sized, ripe bananas, peeled and mashed

3/4 cup plain or vanilla yogurt or sour cream

1/2 to 3/4 cup chopped nuts (optional)

1/2 to 3/4 cup raisins (optional)

Salads, Side Dishes and Vegetables

IN MAYA GASTRONOMIC PRACTICE, with a few exceptions, green salads and vegetable dishes are not the custom. The vegetables are usually incorporated into a main dish and salads are more likely to be part of the garnishes for the *Platos Fuertes* or main dishes. In this section, you will find several salads that can serve as part of a multi-course offering or as a light main dish, some side dishes traditional to the cuisine and some vegetable recipes along with one of the most important garnishes in Yucatán cooking.

Xol-Chon Kek
Jicama-Orange Salad

For the Dressing

1/2 cup sour orange juice OR 3/8 cup lime juice with 2 tablespoons apple cider or other mild vinegar

1 small clove garlic, smashed, peeled and finely minced

1 or 2 serrano chiles, thinly sliced in rounds OR 1/4 habanero chile, finely minced OR 1 to 2 teaspoons habanero sauce (optional)

Generous pinch ground allspice

1 teaspoon orange zest, chopped fine

1 teaspoon honey or sugar

2 tablespoons coarsely chopped cilantro or mint leaves (or a combination of the two)

2 tablespoons olive oil

Salt and pepper, to taste

For the Salad

1 jicama, 12 to 18 ounces, peeled and cut in thin slices, julienne, chunks, or as you prefer

2 to 3 sweet oranges or other citrus, peeled with a knife and sectioned (reserve 1 teaspoon of the zest before peeling)

1 red onion, peeled, rinsed to deflame and thinly sliced

1 sweet red pepper, seeded and thinly sliced (optional)

JICAMA IS A ROOT VEGETABLE NATIVE to Mexico and Latin America with a crunchy texture, similar to water chestnut, and a slightly sweet, nutty flavor. It can be eaten raw or cooked and is a source of vitamin C and potassium. Often sold by street vendors with a little lime and chile powder, in this recipe, it is paired with the sweetness of orange, although you could also use grapefruit, tangerine or blood oranges. This salad provides a crisp, cooling foil to many of the rich and spicy main dishes of the Yucatán peninsula. The jicama can be sliced into various shapes; spears, thin wafers, julienne or chunks, to suit your presentation. The chiles in the dressing are optional to allow pairing with a variety of dishes.

Serves 6 to 8

1. Combine all of the dressing components 15 to 30 minutes before serving.

2. Arrange the salad in a bowl or on a serving platter.

3. Drizzle the dressing over the salad to cover.

4. Serve cool but not overly chilled for the best flavor.

Salpicón de Venado
Venison Salad

For the Meat

1 venison roast, approximately 3 to 3-1/2 pounds

Salt and pepper, to taste

2 tablespoons vegetable oil or lard

1 onion, sliced and pan-roasted

6 cloves garlic, roasted and peeled

2 carrots, peeled and sliced thick

6 bay leaves, toasted

6 whole allspice berries, toasted and lightly crushed

4 to 6 sprigs fresh thyme (optional)

1 tablespoon Mexican oregano, toasted (optional)

1 to 2 tablespoons Recado Colorado (see recipe on page 29), or prepared achiote paste

1/2 cup sour orange juice OR 1/4 cup sweet orange juice with 2 tablespoons mild vinegar

1-1/2 cups water

SALPICÓN IS A FRENCH TERM that when adapted into Mexican cooking usually refers to a cool salad containing cooked items such as meat, seafood or vegetables. This recipe calls for venison, native to the Yucatán peninsula and still very popular throughout the Maya world. The venison is often prepared "Pibil Style" and Salpicón is a good use for leftover Cochinita Pibil (see recipe on page 126); however, the following recipe yields good results and is easier. Of course, beef or pork may be substituted for the venison.

Serves 4 to 6 as a main course or 8 to 10 as a salad course

For the Meat

1. Season the roast with salt and pepper.

2. In a preheated heavy skillet, add the oil and sear the meat well on all sides.

3. Place the meat in a roasting pan and distribute the vegetable and herbs under and on top of the roast.

4. Mix the recado with the liquids and add to the pan, pouring over the meat, cover tightly and place in a 350-degree-F oven.

5. Roast 2 to 2-1/2 hours until very tender. Check the meat halfway through the process, turn it over and redistribute the seasonings and vegetables. Reserve the pan drippings.

6. Cool the roast and shred with a fork or by hand.

For the Salad and Dressing

1. Blanch the carrots and chayotes or potatoes in boiling salted water until al dente. Set aside to cool.

2. To make the dressing, mix the juices, vinegar, pan drippings, salt and pepper together.

3. Combine all the remaining ingredients, including the shredded meat, and toss with the dressing.

4. Serve cool but not overly chilled for best flavor.

For the Salad and Dressing

1 or 2 carrots, sliced

1 or 2 chayotes or waxy potatoes, peeled and sliced

Juice of 2 limes

1/4 cup orange juice

1 tablespoon mild vinegar

1 tablespoon reserved pan drippings

Salt and pepper, to taste

1 medium red onion, peeled and thinly sliced

1/3 cup cilantro leaves

2 tablespoons vegetable or olive oil

Any or all of the following:

Sliced radishes

1 or 2 medium tomatoes, seeded and cut into strips

1 sweet red pepper and/or poblano chile, stemmed seeded and cut into small strips

Frijoles Negros de Olla
Basic Black Beans

3 quarts cold water

1 pound dried beans, sorted for
    rocks, debris and broken beans;
    then well rinsed with cold water

1 medium white onion, roughly
    chopped

2 cloves garlic, crushed and peeled

1 tablespoon lard or vegetable oil

1 or 2 sprigs epazote OR 2 teaspoons
    dried epazote

1-1/2 teaspoons salt

Optional Ingredients:

1 to 2 whole chipotle, jalapeño or
    habanero chiles (By leaving the
    chiles whole, you get a lot of fla-
    vor without all of the heat.
    Beans in Mexico are usually not
    that hot. If you want it hotter,
    chop some of the chile at the end
    of the cooking and mix in
    enough until it suits you.)

2 to 3 fresh or toasted dried avocado
    leaves OR a generous pinch of
    lightly toasted, ground anise seed

1 or 2 Hoja Santa or Acuyo leaves

LITERALLY "BEANS OF THE POT," this is the basic preparation for beans in most of the Maya territories. Although this recipe is for black beans, it applies to all of the available colors and varieties. The beans are often served like this as a side or main dish or used in other recipes.

Regarding the question of soaking the beans or not, I am of the camp that does not. The soaking does speed up the cooking some, but also causes the skins to break and shed more readily. Soaking and changing water several times does help a little with the gassiness associated with bean consumption, nevertheless, if you cook your beans well and also use epazote, you should not have a problem. Also included are some optional additions for extra flavor. Do not forget that the salt and any acidic ingredients should not be added to beans until they are fully cooked. These beans are somewhat brothy and are usually served in a bowl or deep dish.

Makes about 4 cups (6 to 8 servings)

1. Place the water and beans in a large pot (the water should be triple the height of the beans in the pot).

2. Slowly heat to boiling. Reduce the heat to barely boiling and cook for 1 to 1-1/2 hours.

3. Add the onion, garlic and the lard and continue slowly cooking until the beans are completely cooked through, 1-1/2 to 2-1/2 hours, depending on the dryness of the beans, the altitude, the pot you use and your stove. (Beans are done when there is a uniform interior color and soft texture throughout.)

4. Add the epazote, salt and any optional ingredients. Simmer another 15 to 20 minutes, stirring occasionally and adding water, if needed, to prevent burning. The beans will be very soft, creamy in texture and the broth will have thickened to some degree.

5. Serve in a bowl as the beans are brothy, or use as instructed in other recipes.

94

Frijoles Colados Yucatecos
Black Beans Yucatán Style

IN THE YUCATÁN, THE BLACK BEANS are passed through a sieve to remove the skins and make them smooth. This is in contrast to the simply smashed beans, Frijoles Refritos, from other regions of the country. The results are then seared in hot fat, cooked slowly until thick, and served as a side dish, a sauce or a filling for antojitos (snacks).

Makes about 4 cups (6 to 8 servings)

1. Remove the habanero chile and reserve if still intact. Discard the epazote and avocado leaves.

2. Puree the beans in a blender until smooth.

3. Pass through a fine sieve or strainer (if you do not have a strainer that works well for this you may omit this step).

4. In a preheated heavy pot, sauté the onion in the oil with the pinch of salt until color just begins to develop. Add the strained beans and the reserved or a fresh whole habanero chile.

5. Cook on high heat while stirring for 3 to 4 minutes, reduce to medium-low heat, and cook for 10 to 15 minutes more, stirring occasionally until the beans form a thick, but not dry, paste. Add water as needed to prevent burning.

1 recipe Frijoles Negro de Olla (see recipe opposite), using the habanero chile and the avocado leaves or hoja santa or ground anise options

1 small to medium onion, very thinly sliced in strips

1 to 2 tablespoons vegetable oil or lard

Pinch salt

Budín de Chayote
Baked Chayote Squash Pudding

THIS BUDÍN MADE FROM THE CHAYOTE, is an example of the many puddings popular around the Yucatán Peninsula that are made with a variety of vegetables. Budín can be savory or sweet and this recipe goes both ways. Traditionally, the pudding is poured into the shells of the squash and baked, although a casserole dish, individual soufflé cups or a round mold also serve well as baking vessels.

Serves 6 to 8

4 chayotes

1 + 1/2 teaspoon salt

5 eggs

1/4 cup sugar

4 tablespoons butter, melted

1/4 cup flour

1/4 cup cream

Black pepper, to taste

1. Place the chayotes in a pot, cover with water and add 1 teaspoon of salt. Bring to a boil, reduce the heat to simmer and cook for 30 minutes or so until the chayotes are tender.

2. Drain and rinse with water to cool. Slice each chayote in half, remove and discard the seed and scoop out the flesh.

3. Place all of the ingredients in a food processor and puree until smooth.

4. Place the skin halves (if using) in a well-oiled baking dish and fill with the mixture. Bake at 350 degrees F for 30 to 35 minutes, until the budín is firm. Serve hot or cold.

NOTE: *For the sweet version, eliminate the black pepper, double the sugar, then add 1-1/2 teaspoons ground canela and 2 teaspoons vanilla extract to the mixture before baking.*

Contemporary additions: Use a poblano chile and/or a sweet red pepper, roasted, seeded, peeled and cut into strips to decorate the savory version of the budín before baking. You can also top with grated cheese, if desired.

Arroz Amarillo
Yellow Rice

2 teaspoons ground annatto OR
   1 tablespoon Recado Colorado
   (see recipe on page 29)

2-3/4 cups chicken broth or water

1-1/2 cups long-grain rice

2 tablespoons olive oil

1/2 cup diced red onion

4 cloves garlic, sliced

1 poblano chile or 2 jalapeño chiles,
   stemmed, seeded and diced

2 medium tomatoes, charred and
   chopped

1 cup fresh shelled green peas
   (frozen peas my be substituted)

1 sprig fresh epazote OR 2 teaspoons
   dried (1 teaspoon fresh marjoram leaves may be substituted)

1-1/2 teaspoons salt

1/2 teaspoon ground black pepper

THIS IS A GOOD EXAMPLE of Mexican cooking emulating Spanish style while utilizing native ingredients. Instead of saffron, Maya cooks use annatto or achiote to achieve the deep yellow color of Spanish rice. A healthy pinch of saffron could still be used in place of the annatto.

Serves 6 to 8

1. Dissolve the annatto in the broth.

2. Sauté the rice in the oil until it begins to turn opaque. Add the onion, garlic and chiles and fry another minute or two.

3. Add the broth, tomatoes, peas, epazote, salt and pepper.

4. Bring to a boil, stir once to combine well, cover and reduce the heat to simmer.

5. Simmer for 12 minutes; remove from the heat and steam for 15 minutes without removing the cover.

6. Fluff with a spoon or fork and serve.

Cebollas Moradas Encurtidas
Pickled Red Onions

THESE SAVORY, SWEET AND SOUR ONIONS are the ubiquitous garnish for the majority of dishes in the Yucatán cooking repertoire, and their striking color and crunchy texture make a suitable embellishment for many other Maya plates as well. They will keep for several months in the refrigerator, and they may be easily canned for long-term storage.

Makes about 3 cups

1. Place everything except the onions in a nonreactive saucepan. Bring to a boil and cook for 7 minutes. Remove the orange.

2. Put the onions in a bowl, pour the hot mixture over the onions and stir well.

3. NOTE: You may strain the liquid to remove the spices before adding to the onions, if you prefer. I like the rustic quality and added flavor gained by leaving them in.

4. Juice the orange and add the juice to the bowl of onions. Stir again to ensure that the onions are completely submerged. Cool to room temperature, stirring several more times. Refrigerate. (If canning, add the orange juice, skip the cooling, pour into the canning jars and follow canning instructions for heating and sealing.)

NOTE: *Before serving, take the onions out of the refrigerator to allow the onions to warm a little; they taste better at room temperature.*

1 cup mild vinegar such as apple cider, rice or pineapple

1/2 cup sour orange juice or water

1 clove garlic

1 teaspoon whole allspice berries, toasted

2 teaspoons black peppercorns, toasted

4 whole cloves

1 (2-inch) stick canela

4 bay leaves, toasted

1 or 2 sprigs fresh thyme and/or marjoram

1 habanero chile, asado (optional)

2 tablespoons panela or raw sugar

1 tablespoon salt

1 unpeeled orange or tangerine

3 large red onions, peeled and sliced 3/8 to 1/4 inch thick in rounds or strips

Hongos de Chiquin-Te
Wild Mushroom "Polenta"

2 to 3 medium tomatoes (about 6 ounces), charred

1 medium white onion, peeled, sliced and pan-roasted

2 teaspoons Recado Colorado (see recipe on page 29) or prepared achiote condiment

1/2 pound dried tree ear mushrooms, soaked in very hot water until soft and stems removed OR 1 pound assorted fresh wild and domestic mushrooms, all cut into bite-sized pieces

1-1/2 teaspoons salt

3/4 cup masa harina

2 sprigs fresh epazote OR
2 tablespoons dry epazote OR
1 tablespoon fresh oregano leaves

THIS SIDE DISH FROM SAN JUAN CHAMULA, in the hills surrounding San Cristóbal de las Casas, Chiapas, is served along with meat dishes for festivals or used as a vegetarian meat alternative during Lent. The Chiquin-Te mushrooms are a type of "Tree Ear" mushroom similar to the Chinese varieties. The addition of some sharp grated cheese and chopped cilantro just before serving makes a nice contemporary addition.

Serves 4 to 6

1. Puree the tomatoes, onion and recado or achiote in a blender.

2. Place the mushrooms in a pot and add just enough water to cover, bring to a boil and add the salt.

3. While stirring over the heat, mix in the masa little by little until it is smoothly dissolved.

4. Add the tomato mixture and the epazote, stir well, reduce the heat to simmer and cook for 10 minutes, stirring occasionally.

5. Serve immediately.

Ensalada de Rábanos y Chicharrones
Radish and Pork Rind Salad

THIS UNUSUAL COMBINATION FOR A SALAD is a crunchy, crispy, textural celebration to go along with the contrasting flavors of the peppery radishes, rich chicharrones and the acidic citrus. An excellent side dish, this also makes a nice addition to tacos and tostadas, and is delectable as a topping for sliced avocados. When I first sampled this salad, it was prepared using fresh chopped, peppery, anise-like Yerba Santa (also known as Hoja Santa, Acuyo or Root Beer Plant) and, if you can get it, the taste is blissfully exotic; however, the mint and cilantro also do the salad justice.

Makes 4 to 6 servings as a side dish

1. Toss all of the ingredients, except the chicharrones, together and let sit for 15 minutes or so to allow the flavors to blend.

2. Add the chicharrones and toss just before serving.

2 bunches radishes, topped, cleaned and quartered (about 2-1/2 cups)

1/2 cup red onion, diced large and rinsed (see page 19)

1 or 2 serrano or jalapeño chiles, thinly sliced in rounds OR a few dashes of bottled habanero sauce

1/3 cup cilantro and/or mint leaves, chopped

1 tablespoon lime juice

1/4 cup sour orange juice OR 1/8 cup sweet orange juice plus 1 tablespoon mild vinegar

1-1/2 teaspoons salt

1 tablespoon vegetable or olive oil

1-1/2 cups chicharrones (crispy fried pork rinds, the Mexican varieties are the best), cut into bite-sized pieces

Rice and Beans

1 cup dry red or black beans (2 well-drained cans of cooked beans may be substituted)

4 cups water (to cook the beans)

1-1/2 tablespoons vegetable oil

2 tablespoons chopped white onion

1/4 cup chopped sweet red or green pepper

1 teaspoon minced jalapeño or serrano chile OR 1 whole habanero chile (do not break the skin of the chile or it will make the dish way too hot)

2 cloves garlic, smashed and peeled

1-1/4 cups long-grained rice (not converted)

1 teaspoon chopped fresh thyme OR 1/2 teaspoon dried

1 teaspoon salt

1/2 teaspoon black pepper

1 (13-ounce) can unsweetened coconut milk (1-1/2 cups)

1/2 cup water

Chopped cilantro for garnish (optional)

THIS RECIPE COMES FROM THE MAYAN-INHABITED areas of the Yucatán, Quintana Roo and Guatemala. The name is usually listed in English even on menus otherwise written entirely in Spanish. The reason for this is that several years ago, many Mayan people fled to English-speaking Belize to escape persecution in their homeland. While there, they assimilated many of the foods from Belize into their repertoire of cooking. This style of cooking the beans and rice together remained popular as an inexpensive main course upon their return to their native soil. As a side dish, this is perfect to go along with grilled entrees and with the addition of bacon, ham hocks or smoked pig's feet it makes for a hearty casual main dish.

Serves 4 as a main course or 6 to 8 as a side dish

1. Cook the dry beans in 4 cups of water until completely cooked through. Drain.

2. In a preheated, heavy saucepan, Dutch oven or deep skillet, add the oil, then fry the onion, peppers, chile and garlic for 1 minute, stirring well. Add the rice and continue to cook for 2 minutes, stirring constantly. When the rice has begun to turn opaque with a little browning, add the thyme, salt, pepper, coconut milk and 1/2 cup water.

3. Bring to a boil and add the beans, stirring to mix.

4. Cover tightly, reduce the heat to simmer and cook 15 minutes more. Remove from the heat, leave the lid on and steam for 15 minutes more. Stir gently to mix and serve. Add cilantro as garnish.

Soups and Stews

SOUPS AND STEWS PLAY AN IMPORTANT role in Maya cooking. Whether served as an appetite-stimulating early course at comida, the central focus of a *cena*, or light supper, or as meals unto themselves, soups and stews reflect the complex flavors of the cuisine, are convenient to prepare in advance and often utilize leftovers from previous meals.

Sopa de Lima
Mexican Lime Soup

1 pound chicken pieces

1-1/2 quarts chicken broth

1 habanero or other hot chile,
    charred and left whole

2 tablespoons Recado Salpimentado
    (see recipe on page 33)

4 corn tortillas, cut into thin strips

Oil for frying the tortilla strips

2 tablespoons vegetable oil

1 medium red or white onion,
    chopped or thinly sliced

1 sweet bell pepper (red or green),
    chopped or sliced

3/4 cup diced tomatoes

1 lima or substitute lime, sliced

1 tablespoon fresh lime juice

Chopped cilantro to garnish

Lime wedges

Chile Tumulado, Xnipec (see recipes
    on pages 49 and 40) or other hot
    salsa

ONE OF THE MOST RECOGNIZED menu items in the Yucatán, Sopa de Lima captures the culinary soul of this region. It is at once spicy, flavorful and light, nonetheless satisfying. A soup of this type makes perfect sense in the tropics; the hot broth and spicy habanero chiles actually serve to reduce body temperature, a welcome relief in a hot and steamy climate. The limes here are not the limes we get in U.S. supermarkets. They are more acidic and less sweet; Persian, Mexican/key limes or Meyer lemons work well in this recipe as a substitute.

6 servings

1. Place the chicken pieces in the broth and bring to a boil. Skim any foam that rises to the surface and discard. Add the charred chile and the recado, reduce the heat, cover and cook until the chicken is done (about 30 minutes). Remove the chicken from the broth, cool, pick the meat off the bones, and shred. Strain the broth and reserve.

2. Fry the tortilla strips in the oil until golden brown and drain on paper towels.

3. Add the 2 tablespoons of vegetable oil to a hot, deep skillet, heavy saucepan or Dutch oven and sauté the onion and pepper until softened (3 to 4 minutes). Add the tomatoes and cook for 3 to 4 minutes more while stirring. Add the lime slices and juice, broth and shredded chicken, briefly bring to a boil, reduce the heat and simmer for 12 minutes. Adjust for salt.

4. Ladle into warmed bowls and garnish with the tortilla strips and chopped cilantro. Pass the lime wedges and hot salsa.

Crema de Aguacate
Avocado Soup

BOTH HOT AND COLD VERSIONS of this soup are found around the Yucatán. This recipe may be used either way. I use the cold version as an appetizer or palate cleanser in a multi-course meal and serve it warm with some crispy bacon crumbles or chicharrones (pork rinds) along with some white rice as a light supper or lunch entree.

Serves 4 to 6

1. Sauté the onion in the oil until soft, clear and just beginning to brown. Add the diced tomato and fry for 2 minutes more.

2. Add the chile, garlic, ground avocado leaves or anise seed along with the chicken broth and bring to a boil. Reduce heat and simmer for 10 minutes.

3. Peel, pit and coarsely chop the avocados and add to the broth with the cream and lime juice.

4. Puree in a blender, adjust for salt and pepper and serve warm with your choice of garnishes or chill to serve cold later.

NOTE: *After chilling, reheat the soup gently to serve it warm, it will burn easily and may separate with extended cooking.*

1/2 cup chopped white onion

1 tablespoon vegetable oil

1/2 cup tomato, charred, then chopped

1 or 2 serrano, yellow hot, New Mexico green or jalapeño chiles OR 1/2 chile habanero, well charred and seeded

4 cloves garlic, roasted and peeled

2 to 3 Mexican avocado leaves, toasted and ground OR 1/4 teaspoon toasted and ground anise seed

3-1/2 cups chicken broth

3 large ripe avocados (Hass is the preferred variety)

1/3 cup light cream or half-and-half

1 tablespoon lime juice

Salt and pepper, to taste

Garnish suggestions: Chopped cilantro, thinly sliced radishes, tortilla chips, chicharrones, crumbled bacon, pickled red onions, lime slices and sour cream or Mexican crema

Yucatán Meat and Vegetable Stew

1-1/2 pounds beef chuck roast or stew meat cut in 1-1/2-inch pieces

1 white onion, peeled, sliced in thirds and pan-roasted, then chopped

12 cloves garlic, roasted, then peeled

3 quarts beef or chicken broth or water

1-1/2 pounds pork shoulder, leg or stew meat cut into 1-1/2-inch pieces

1 recipe Recado Adobo Blanco o de Puchero (see recipe on page 34)

1 fryer-sized chicken, or about 3 pounds bone-in turkey, cut into serving-sized pieces

Vegetable suggestions
(usually the vegetables are cooked and served in large pieces)

Carrots, peeled

Chayotes, quartered

Sweet potatoes or yams, cut lengthwise

Kohlrabi

Winter squash like acorn, butternut, etc.

Potatoes, halved or quartered lengthwise

A TRUE FIESTA CLASSIC, *Puchero* is the Spanish word for stew. Its large quantities serve many guests and a huge pot is required to prepare it. The Maya have co-opted this dish by adding their distinctive flavors. The Maya word *pux* or *puch* means to mash and many still do mash the vegetables together after they are cooked; however, it is more typical these days to see the vegetables served whole on the side along with the three meats, beef, pork and chicken or turkey, to give the guests a choice. *Arroz con Fideos* (rice and vermicelli) is traditionally cooked in with the Puchero, although many prefer it on the side. To do this, simply add some of the puchero broth to the sautéed rice and pasta and cook it in a covered pan, separate from the stew. You may also prepare the Puchero without the rice and pasta. The vegetable options are almost endless; the recipe contains suggestions that you may freely add to as you like or depending on what is available. Be careful that you add them in a timed order that will allow for them to finish cooking at the same time.

Serves 8 to 12, depending on the amount of vegetables used

1. Put the beef in a large pot with the onion, garlic and the 3 quarts of broth or water. Bring to a boil, cover, and reduce heat to simmer and cook for 1 hour. Add the pork, re-cover and cook for 30 additional minutes.

2. Add the recado and the chicken pieces, bring back to a boil, cover again, reduce heat to simmer and cook for 45 more minutes. Periodically check and skim off any foam and excess fat that rises.

3. Place the vegetables to cook at the appropriate time so that they will be ready together.

4. When the vegetables are almost done, in a separate skillet, heat the oil and sauté the rice and stir well until it begins to turn opaque. Using a

(continued on page 114)

Plantains, green and unpeeled, cut
    in sections

Cabbage

Corn on the cob, in sections

Garbanzo or white beans

Green peas

Green beans

Tomato wedges

2 to 3 tablespoons vegetable oil

3/4 to 1 cup rice

8 ounces fideos or vermicelli, broken
    into small pieces

1 lime, cut in half

Garnishes

Salpicón de Rábanos (see recipe on
    page 48)

Chopped cilantro

Diced hot chiles

Xnipec or salsas chili Tumulado
    (see recipes on pages 40 and 49)

Lime wedges

Sliced avocados

slotted spoon, remove the rice from the pan and add to the Puchero pot. Repeat with the pasta and also add to the pot after the rice has been in for about 12 to 15 minutes.

5. When the fideos are soft, turn off the heat and put the lime halves in to scent the Puchero for a few minutes before serving.

6. Remove the meat and vegetables and arrange on a platter.

7. Serve the Puchero in bowls and allow the guests to place the meat, vegetables and garnishes as they like.

Caldo de Venado
Venison Soup

THE SMALL RED DEER has been a staple in the Maya Yucatán since pre-Hispanic days and is still hunted in the wild as well as raised domestically by some families. Since it is becoming scarce, many cooks now use beef as a substitute. Variations include the addition of cooked vegetables like yams, chayote squash, corn, red or white beans, potatoes and carrots just before serving.

Serves 6 to 8

1. Dissolve the recados in the sour orange juice. Blend the masa harina with 3/4 cup of the broth or water until smooth and set aside.

2. Season the meat with salt and pepper. In a preheated soup kettle, heavy pot or Dutch oven, add the oil and brown the meat on high heat.

3. Strain the Chiltomate into the meat and fry, while stirring, for 2 to 3 minutes.

4. Add the orange juice with the recados and the masa paste along with the remaining broth. Bring to a boil, cover, reduce heat to simmer and cook for 1-1/2 to 2 hours, until the meat is fork-tender.

5. Add the red onions and chile rings and cook for 10 minutes more, adjust the seasonings and serve with the garnishes.

3 tablespoons Recado Colorado (see recipe on page 29)

1 tablespoon Recado de Bistec (see recipe on page 31) OR 6 fresh epazote leaves (1-1/2 tablespoons dried) and 1/2 teaspoon ground, toasted coriander seeds

2/3 cup sour orange juice OR 1/2 cup sweet orange juice with 2 tablespoons mild vinegar

1/4 cup masa harina

Approximately 2 quarts beef or chicken broth or water, to cover

3 to 3-1/2 pounds venison or lean beef, cut into 1-inch cubes

Salt and pepper, to taste

3 tablespoons vegetable oil or lard

1 recipe Chiltomate (see recipe on page 44), blended smooth

1 medium red onion, slivered

3 to 4 xcatic, guero, yellow hot or Anaheim chiles, sliced in rings

Fresh chopped cilantro, radish slices and lime wedges to garnish

Potage de Ibes
White Beans with Pork

ANOTHER ONE-DISH MEAL, this satisfying stew is usually made with white beans (ibes), although many other varieties are acceptable: lima beans, red beans, pinto beans, black-eyed peas or black beans. Vegetables such as chayotes, sweet potatoes, yams, white potatoes, squash, etc., may be added as you like.

Serves 4 to 6

1. Cook the beans in water to cover until beginning to soften (about 1 hour or 15 minutes in a pressure cooker).

2. Add the pork and epazote and continue cooking until the beans are done and the pork is tender. Drain and reserve 1 cup of the cooking liquid.

3. Sauté the onion and longaniza (if using) in the oil until beginning to brown, add the garlic, chile and tomatoes and cook for 1 to 2 minutes more. Add the recado, season with salt and pepper and simmer until the tomatoes are soft.

4. Combine the beans and pork, reserved cooking liquid and the seasoning fritanga and simmer 15 minutes to combine the flavors and thicken it a little. Adjust for salt and serve.

Garnish with chopped cilantro; red onions (raw or pickled); toasted, ground pumpkinseeds; chopped boiled eggs; and lime wedges.

1 pound small white beans

1/2 pound pork shoulder or leg, cut in 1-inch squares

1 sprig fresh OR 1 tablespoon dry epazote

1 medium white onion, diced

1/2 pound Longaniza (see recipe on page 63) or chorizo, cut in bite-sized pieces (optional)

1-1/2 tablespoons vegetable oil

6 cloves garlic, roasted and peeled

1 habanero chile OR 2 to 3 jalapeño or serrano chiles, charred and left intact

1 cup diced tomatoes

1-1/2 tablespoons Recado Colorado (see recipe on page 29), dissolved in 3 tablespoons sour orange juice or 2 tablespoons mild vinegar

Salt and pepper, to taste

Cremas de Cilantro y Elotes
Sweet Corn and Cilantro Cream Soups

1 leek (white part only), sliced

2 carrots, peeled and sliced

1 medium white onion, sliced

4 cloves garlic, peeled and halved lengthwise

2 stalks celery, diced

1/4 pound butter

1 or 2 poblano chiles, New Mexico green chiles or jalapeños, roasted, peeled, stemmed, seeded and diced

3 tablespoons flour, divided

1 quart chicken or vegetable broth, divided

2 cups milk, divided

3 ears of corn, char-grilled or boiled until tender, then stripped off the cob OR 2 cups frozen corn kernels (thawed)

1 quart heavy cream, divided

Salt and pepper, to taste

Leaves and tops from 2 large bunches cilantro

THIS TWO-PART SOUP USES the Mexican favorite *Crema de Elotes* alongside the Yucatán *Crema de Cilantro* to create a striking side-by-side presentation. If you prefer, for simplicity, the two soups may be combined and cooked together as one; the flavors combine well.

Serves 8

1. Slowly cook the leek, carrots, onion, garlic and celery in the butter until tender. Add the chiles and divide equally into 2 pots.

2. In the first pot, add 1 tablespoon of the flour and cook for 1 minute while stirring. Add 1/2 of the broth, continuing to stir until all of the flour is smoothly dissolved. Add 1 cup of milk and the corn. Simmer for 12 to 15 minutes. Add 1 cup of the cream and heat through. Puree smooth in a blender and strain back into the pot. Season with salt and pepper and simmer 5 more minutes.

3. In the second pot, add 2 tablespoons of the flour and cook for 1 minute while stirring. Add the remaining broth, continuing to stir until all of the flour is smoothly dissolved; add 1 cup of milk. Simmer for 12 to 15 minutes, add 2 cups of the cream and heat through.

4. Puree the last cup of cream with the cilantro and add it to the pot. Mix together, then puree it all smooth in the blender and strain into the pot. Season with salt and pepper and simmer 5 more minutes.

5. To serve, place side by side in a bowl using two gravy boats, pitchers or ladles at the same time.

Meat

THE EXTENSIVE USE OF DOMESTICATED ANIMALS in the diet of the Maya people is a relative new development. Prior to the arrival of the Spanish, the main source of meat was hunting and often that bounty of the jungle was reserved for the elite rulers and religious leaders. In contemporary Maya culture, beef and especially pork has become something that is consumed daily for many, especially in urban zones. In less affluent locales, the consumption of red meat may be limited to once or twice a week and for important festivals and celebrations. Meat has been added in small quantities to enrich and improve the nutritional value of many previously vegetarian recipes. In the following recipes you will experience a cross section of meat dishes from around the Maya lands, and the techniques and flavor combinations should guide you into creating your own recipes for meats prepared in the Maya style.

X'alben Ti'bal-Carne Ahumada de Tenejapa
Smoked Pork Loin

1 ounce Recado Colorado (see recipe on page 29) OR 1 cube commercial achiote paste

2 tablespoons sour orange or lime juice or cider vinegar

1 teaspoon salt

1/2 teaspoon black pepper

1 teaspoon toasted and ground allspice

2 pounds pork tenderloin (peeled) or boneless pork loin, cut into 1x1-inch-thick strips, 8 to 10 inches long

1/2 pound (about 3 to 4) small tomatoes

1 small white onion, peeled

3 chiles guajillos, puyas or New Mexican reds or other hot dried chiles, as you like

2 corn tortillas

1 tablespoon vegetable oil or pork lard

5 to 6 fresh epazote leaves or 1-1/2 tablespoons dried or 1/4 cup cilantro leaves

Salt, to taste

Water as needed

THIS SIMPLE DISH IS A FEAST DAY specialty of the village Tenejapa, in the hills surrounding San Cristóbal de las Casas, Chiapas. There the indigenous of Tenejapa usually use the tougher cuts of pork like shoulder or leg, slice it wafer-thin to make tasajo and smoke it until it is dried like jerky. For this recipe, I have chosen to use pork tenderloin and cut it thicker creating a more contemporary version; however, you could use the original cuts, sliced very thin, and smoke them until almost dried to re-create the traditional. Served with freshly made tortillas, chayote or squash and some sliced avocado, X'alben Ti'bal makes an especially satisfying feast.

Serves 4 to 6

1. Mix 1/2 of the recado with the sour orange juice, salt, black pepper and ground allspice.

2. Rub the mixture all over the cuts of pork and set aside to marinate 30 to 60 minutes.

3. In a heavy skillet, saucepan or comal, roast and char the tomatoes, onion and chiles. Remove from the pan, de-stem, and seed the chiles.

4. Toast the tortillas over high heat in the same pan until they are dark brown, almost black.

5. Puree the tomatoes, chiles, onions and the remaining recado with enough water to make a smooth paste.

6. Place the marinated pork in a smoker and smoke on medium low (about 275 degrees F) for about 35 to 45 minutes until the meat is cooked through, yet still moist. NOTE: you may also char-grill the pork until cooked about medium (5 to 6 minutes per side). Cover and set aside.

7. Heat the oil on high in a heavy saucepan or deep skillet, add the puree and fry for about 2 minutes, stirring constantly. Add the epazote, reduce the heat to simmer and add salt and additional water as needed.

8. Add the smoked meat (either in whole pieces or you may cut them in bite-sized slices) and simmer for 10 minutes more. Serve hot.

Cochito al Horno
Oven-Baked Pork

3 pounds pork shoulder, pork belly (uncured) or pork sirloin

2 pounds fresh pig's feet, or 1 rack of baby back or spare ribs, separated

Water or meat broth

6 ancho chiles

3 guajillo or New Mexican red chiles

1 cup mild vinegar

10 whole peppercorns

6 whole cloves

4 whole allspice berries

3 (2-inch) sticks canela

1 tablespoon whole mustard seed

Generous pinch dried thyme

Generous pinch Mexican oregano

2 tablespoons sugar

3 ripe tomatoes (about 1/2 pound)

3 green tomatoes or 4 tomatillos

1/2 white onion, peeled and chopped

10 cloves garlic, peeled

3 tablespoons lard or vegetable oil

5 bay leaves

1 (3-inch) piece fresh gingerroot, peeled and cut into 5 slices

Salt, to taste

THIS *GUISO, OR STEW, IS FROM* the Maya Tzotzil Village of Simojovel, Chiapas, but is a good example of *comida mestiza*, or food from a mixed Spanish and indigenous heritage. It is full of aromatic spices and herbs and achieves an amazing richness from using pig's feet; however, pork ribs may be substituted for the pig's feet or a rich meat stock may be used to cook the pork chunks instead of water. Cochita al Horno is a festive dish usually served as the main course, although the tender chunks of meat serve well as a filling for tacos, empanadas and other corn-based antojitos.

Serves 6 to 8 as a main course

1. Pound pork to help tenderize and cut into approximately 1-1/2-inch-square pieces. Season the meat and pigs feet or ribs with salt and place in a heavy pan and cover with water or broth. Bring to a boil, cover and cook for 25 minutes. Note: You can substitute a rich meat stock or broth for the water in the recipe if eliminating this ingredient.

2. Remove the meat and reserve the liquid.

3. Toast the chiles (see page 24), remove the stems and seeds and soak in the vinegar for 15 minutes.

4. Lightly toast the dry spices and herbs, and blend together with the vinegar from the soaking chiles. Add sugar, tomatoes, chiles, onion and garlic.

5. Heat the lard or oil in an ovenproof casserole or Dutch oven. Brown the meat well and add the tomato-chile-spice mixture. Continue stirring for about 2 more minutes.

6. Add the bay leaves, ginger slices, a dash of salt and enough of the cooking liquid to cover (about 4 to 5 cups). Stir well to mix, cover and place in a 350-degree-F oven and bake for 1 to 1-1/2 hours until the meat is tender.

 *Olla Podrida*

Rich Man's Beans

LITERALLY TRANSLATED, *Olla Podrida* means fermented cooking pot, hardly an appetizing moniker. In this recipe's name; however, it is a Latin American colloquialism that refers to being rich or the ability to afford these rich ingredients. This dish is similar to the *Frijoles Charros* of northern Mexico's cattle country. Typically a fiesta dish, you may serve Olla Podrida as a hearty, informal main dish or as a side dish in a multi-course meal.

Serves 6 to 8 as a main course

1. Cook the beans in water until cooked through. Drain the liquid from the beans until it is the same level as the beans.

2. Puree the tomatoes, guajillo chiles, onion and garlic in a blender.

3. Cut the meat in bite-sized pieces. In a heavy pot, sauté the pieces of meat in the pork lard until lightly browned (about 5 minutes), add the tomato-onion-chile pure and continue frying 2 more minutes while stirring.

4. Add the beans and the pork rinds. Bring to a boil, reduce the heat and simmer for 25 minutes.

5. Add the epazote and serrano chiles and simmer for 15 additional minutes. Adjust for salt.

2 pounds, white, red or black beans

2 medium tomatoes (about 8 ounces)

2 guajillo or 3 ancho chiles, toasted, stemmed, seeded and soaked (see page 24)

1 medium white onion

6 cloves garlic

6 ounces beef jerky (cecina de res)

8 ounces pork chorizo

8 ounces Longaniza (see recipe on page 63), or other smoked sausage (thick-sliced bacon, cut into cubes and cooked until most of the fat has been rendered could also be substituted here)

2 tablespoons pork lard or vegetable oil

8 ounces pork rinds (chicharrónes)

1 or 2 sprigs epazote OR 1 tablespoon dried epazote OR 1 tablespoon toasted Mexican oregano

4 or 5 pickled serrano chiles, split in half lengthwise

Salt, to taste

Cochinita Pibil
Pit-Roasted Pork with Yucatán Spices

1 medium, boneless pork butt or
arm roast (4-1/2 to 6-1/2
pounds), trimmed but with some
fat remaining

4 tablespoons Recado Colorado (see
recipe on page 29)

12 cloves garlic, peeled

1 medium white onion, coarsely
chopped (3/4 cup)

2 tablespoons whole allspice berries,
toasted and cracked OR 1 tablespoon ground allspice

2 tablespoons Mexican oregano,
toasted

1 teaspoon cumin seed, toasted and
crushed

2 teaspoons cracked black pepper

6 bay leaves, toasted

2 tablespoons Worcestershire sauce,
optional (not traditional, but I
did learn the trick in Mexico)

3/4 cup sour orange juice OR 1/2
cup sweet orange juice + 1 tablespoon mild, fruity vinegar

1/4 cup mild, fruity vinegar

2 to 3 fresh habanero or Scotch
bonnet chiles, stems and seeds
removed, OR 2 to 3 tablespoons
bottled habanero chile sauce

THIS IS PROBABLY THE MOST WELL-KNOWN food in the Yucatán. From resorts to city restaurants, street vendors to family gatherings and fiestas, Cochinita Pibil and its cousin, Pollo Pibil, are both revered and enjoyed frequently. I have included a recipe for Cochinita Pibil in my previous two cookbooks, so it is safe to assume that it is important for me also. It is the number-one choice for my family gatherings and celebrations with friends and, as a chef and consultant, I have successfully installed it on several restaurant menus. The dish is relatively simple to prepare and has maximum impact with its rich flavors and exotic aromas all encased in a banana leaf.

Pibil is the Mayan word for a pit that is dug in the ground, then lined with stones to roast a suckling pig. A fire is built and allowed to burn for several hours until it has been reduced to smoldering coals. Meanwhile, the *cochinita*, or little pig, has been seasoned and marinated with the exotic flavors of the brick-red achiote, the bright taste of citrus and the floral heat of the habanero chile. Wrapped in banana leaves, the meat is placed in the pit, covered with the rocks and some palm leaves or wet burlap, and slow roasted overnight. This feast is then served family style with fresh handmade tortillas, salsas, condiments and salads to make your own tacos. Cochinita Pibil is a celebratory meal, excellent for parties and gatherings; the long, unattended cooking period allows time in the kitchen for the preparation of salsas, condiments and side dishes. While long, slow cooking in an actual wood-fired pit is certainly the ultimate method for this recipe, roasting in the oven or slowly on a BBQ grill will produce stellar results. Although the banana leaves lend a distinct flavor to the meat as well as a dramatic presentation, a package of aluminum foil instead of the leaves also results in an outstanding dish. Try cooking the Cochinita a day or two in advance, then make individual serving packets, wrapped in banana leaves, and heat them on a char grill just before serving.

Makes around 3-1/2 to 4-1/2 pounds of cooked pork

(enough for 8 to 10 main courses or 42 to 48 tacos)

1. Make several one-inch-deep cuts on the fat side of the pork to allow the marinade to penetrate. Place the meat in a freezer bag or other large plastic bag or a large nonreactive container.

2. Puree all the other ingredients except banana leaves in a blender. Pour in with the pork, seal bag and distribute well to coat the meat. Marinate at least 2 hours or overnight in the refrigerator.

3. Preheat oven to 325 degrees F.

4. Toast the banana leaves to make them more pliable (see page 19). Line the bottom of a heavy roasting pan with 2 or 3 of the banana leaves. They should overlap the pan on all sides.

5. Remove the pork roast from the bag and reserve the marinade.

6. Place pork fat side up on banana leaves in the pan. Pour about 1/2 cup of the marinade over top of the meat. NOTE: You may want to place the package that is wrapped in banana leaves on a sheet of aluminum foil to catch any leaks.

7. Place 3 or 4 more leaves over the pork and inside the bottom leaves. Pull bottom leaves around the meat; tie strips of banana leaves around this package from both directions to secure.

8. Bake at 325 degrees F for 4 to 5 hours until meat is fork tender. Leaves will be darkened on the outside when finished.

9. Allow to cool for 20 minutes, then slit open banana leaves with a sharp knife or scissors (be careful of the steam) and remove the pork or present on the leaves.

Condiment suggestions: Fresh Corn Tortillas (see recipe on page 72), chopped cilantro, citrus wedges, Xnipek salsa (see recipe on page 40), Cebollas Moradas Encutidas (see recipe on page 99), Salpicón de Rábanos (see recipe on page 48), Guacamole (see recipe on page 57), Rice and Beans (see recipe on page 104), or Frijoles Negros de Olla (see recipe on page 94) and Xol-Chon Kek (see recipe on page 90).

2 tablespoons vegetable oil

2 tablespoons salt

1 package (1 pound) frozen banana leaves (available at specialty food stores and Latin American or Asian grocers). Thaw and rinse well in cool water. Tear 8 half-inch-wide strips off one leaf and tie two together to make 4 strips to use later for ties OR use heavy-duty aluminum foil

Queso Relleno
Pork-Stuffed Baked Gouda Cheese

For the Picadillo Filling

2 pounds ground pork or pork butt or shoulder cut into 2-inch chunks

1 onion, quartered

2 cloves garlic

1-1/2 tablespoons Recado de Bistec (see recipe on page 31) made with epazote or add 1 sprig fresh epazote or 1 tablespoon dried epazote

1 teaspoon salt

1 onion, finely chopped

3 cloves garlic, roasted, peeled and chopped

1 sweet pepper or mild chile, seeded and chopped

4 tablespoons pork lard or vegetable oil

1/2 to 1 teaspoon ground canela

1/4 teaspoon ground cloves

4 to 6 whole allspice berries, toasted and ground

5 to 6 tomatoes (3/4 pound), lightly roasted, peeled, seeded and chopped

2 ounces raisins or currants

2 ounces almonds, lightly toasted, peeled and slivered

2 ounces green, pimento-stuffed olives, chopped

IN DAYS PAST, THE YUCATÁN PENINSULA actually had more trade with Europe than with the rest of Mexico, and the preference for many European products like Dutch cheeses is still evident today in Mérida, the capital, and the surrounding towns and villages. The Spanish and Creole influence is demonstrated in the picadillo and the gravy sauce. This recipe is my interpretation of the *Queso Relleno* that I tasted in Silvio Campo's fonda restaurant across from the mercado in the Mayan town of Tixkokob, about an hour from Mérida. This well-known specialty is a Sunday favorite all around the peninsula. Often served as an appetizer, Queso Relleno makes a filling main dish.

Serves 6 to 8

1. Cover the meat with 4 cups of water and bring to a boil with the onion, garlic cloves, recado and salt to taste. Lower the flame and cook for about 30 minutes (or 1-1/4 hours or until tender, if using chunks of meat). Strain the meat, remove the onion and garlic and discard (shred if using chunks of meat), and set the broth aside to cool.

2. Fry the chopped onion, chopped garlic and sweet pepper in the lard until soft but not brown.

3. Add the spices, tomatoes, raisins, almonds, olives and capers and fry another minute.

4. Add the vinegar and the meat and continue to cook until almost dry.

5. Adjust for salt and pepper, stir in the chopped eggs and set aside.

For the Gravy

1. Heat the lard or butter in a skillet or saucepan until it begins to sizzle. Whisk in the flour a little at a time until a smooth paste is formed. Continue stirring while cooking for about 1 minute until a toasty aroma develops.

2. Remove from heat and whisk in the cool pork broth until smooth. Add the onion, tomato, cloves, cumin and saffron. Return to heat and bring to a slow boil. Cook for about 5 minutes until thickened and smooth. Adjust for salt and pepper, and puree if desired.

For the Tomato Sauce

1. Fry the pepper in the lard until soft but not brown.

2. Add the Chiltomate and fry for 2 to 3 minutes more.

3. Add the water, capers and epazote; cook until the sauce has thickened. Remove the epazote. Season with salt and pepper. Blend smooth, if desired.

---

2 tablespoons capers, drained

1/4 cup mild vinegar

Salt and freshly ground black pepper, to taste

3 hard-boiled eggs, chopped

For the Gravy
2 ounces lard or butter

1/4 cup all-purpose flour

1 quart reserved pork broth

1/2 onion, finely minced and browned

1 tomato, charred, peeled, seeded and finely chopped

Pinch ground cloves

Pinch ground cumin

Pinch saffron (optional)

Salt and pepper, to taste

For the Tomato Sauce
1 sweet pepper or mild green or yellow chile (in the Yucatán, chile xcatic or güeros would be used), finely chopped

2 tablespoons pork lard or vegetable oil

1 recipe Chiltomate (see recipe on page 44)

1/2 cup water

129

1 tablespoon capers, drained

2 to 3 leaves fresh epazote (optional)

Salt and pepper, to taste

For the Relleno

1 large round or 6 to 8 small (for individual servings) Gouda or Edam cheese

Banana leaves or cheesecloth to wrap the cheese

For the Relleno

Pare off the red waxy skin with a sharp knife or peeler. Cut a 1/2-inch-thick slice off the top to make a lid. Hollow out the inside of the cheese (a melon ball tool is helpful for this) until the shell is about 1/2 inch thick. Place the picadillo stuffing in the cheese and replace the lid. Wrap the cheese in the banana leaves or cheesecloth, tie it tightly with twine or thread and heat in a bain-marie or double boiler in a preheated oven at 350 degrees F for approximately 35 minutes.

NOTE: *You can improvise the bain-marie by placing a covered roasting pan or casserole in a larger pan containing 1 inch of water.*

Unwrap the cheese, place it on a serving dish and pour first the gravy then the tomato sauce over and around it. This can be served either as a main course, with tortillas for making tacos or as an appetizer. Serve with Chile Tumulado salsa (see recipe on page 49).

Comida Para Todos Santos
All Saints' Day Smoked Pork Stew

This fiesta dish is served on All Saints' Day in the Tzetzal villages in the highlands surrounding San Cristóbal de las Casas Chiapas. This day is also the observance of the Dia de los Muertos, or Day of the Dead, when special foods are prepared to entice the dearly departed to return for a visit. The pork is generally smoked up to a week in advance and then combined with the remaining ingredients to produce a guisada, or stew. The squash that is used in Chiapas is called chilcayote. It is a large green squash with a light-colored interior, and a texture similar to spaghetti squash. You can substitute any firm, winter types here. You may also substitute country-style pork ribs for the pork loin. The seasoning approach to the meat is my own addition; tradition calls for merely washing and heavily salting the meat prior to smoking, but I prefer the flavor achieved by using a recado to marinate it. This dish is traditionally prepared in enormous quantities for the celebration, but I have created a recipe that is a little more manageable.

Serves 6 to 8

1. Combine the recado, salt and vinegar into a paste and rub it over the surface of the meat. Refrigerate covered for 3 hours or overnight.

2. Slow smoke the meat for 2 to 3 hours until cooked through. NOTE: If you are not set up for smoking, bake the meat covered in a 325-degree-F oven for 1-1/2 hours.

3. Place the meat in the center of a roasting pan and arrange the vegetables and cilantro around it.

4. Combine the chile powder, salt and water and pour over everything.

5. Cover and bake at 325 degrees F for 1-1/2 hours.

4 ounces Recado Colorado or Recado de Bistec (see recipes on pages 29 and 31)

2 teaspoons salt

2 tablespoons apple cider or other mild vinegar

1 center cut boneless pork loin 3-1/2 to 4-1/2 pounds

1 cabbage, cored and cut into eighths

6 to 8 medium red potatoes, washed and skin left on

2 pounds chayote, spaghetti, acorn, butternut or other firm squash, cut in 2-inch sections and seeds removed (leave the skin on)

1 white onion, peeled and quartered

3 to 4 ripe tomatoes, cored and quartered

6 cloves garlic, peeled

1 bunch trimmed cilantro

1/2 to 3/4 cup mild to medium chile powder, toasted, OR 1 cup puree from toasted and reconstituted guajillo and ancho chiles (see page 23)

1-1/2 teaspoons salt

1-1/2 quarts water or meat broth

Poc Chuc
Yucatán Grilled Pork

1 tablespoon Recado de Bistec or Recado de Escabeche (see recipes on pages 31 and 32)

1 cup sour orange juice OR 1/2 cup sweet orange juice with 5 tablespoons mild vinegar

2-1/2 pounds pork leg or loin sliced 1/4 inch thick

1 large red onion, cut in eighths and pan-roasted

1/3 cup cilantro leaves, coarsely chopped

2 medium tomatoes, charred and cut into bite-sized pieces

ALTHOUGH CULINARY HISTORY TELLS US that this dish predates the establishment by many years, the original Los Almendros restaurant in Ticul claims to have invented it; however, they have done much for popularizing it with both tourists and locals. The words *Poc Chuc* together mean char-grilled, a typical Maya approach to cooking. Whoever actually invented it did us all a great service. The Los Almendros method, employed by many other restaurants as well, is to slice the pork thinly, marinate and then grill, providing a lot of surface area to caramelize over the hot coals, but this cooking style is also often used for *chuletas*, or pork chops. The first method also cuts the meat into pieces and tosses it with charred and pickled onions, tomatoes and more sour orange juice. If preparing pork chops, just forego those two ingredients.

Serves 4 to 6

1. Dissolve the recado in 3/4 of the juice and marinate the meat in it for 1 hour.

2. Peel the roasted red onion, cut into bite-sized pieces and toss with the remaining juice and cilantro.

3. Char-grill the pork over hot coals or a grill set to high, until the meat is well colored and a little crispy around the edges.

4. Cut the meat into 1-inch squares and toss with the onions and tomatoes.

5. Serve immediately.

Serve with Frijoles Negros de Olla (see recipe on page 94), Chiltomate (see recipe on page 44), Xnipec or Chile Tumulado salsa (see recipes on pages 40 and 49), Cebollas Moradas Encurtidas (see recipe on page 99), sliced avocados and warm corn tortillas.

Frijol con Puerco
Pork with Black Beans

THIS DISH IS SO INGRAINED into the psyche of the people of the Yucatán that every Monday on restaurant menus and home tables throughout the region, you will find Frijol con Puerco. The name is deceptively simple; although the actual process is not too complicated, the presentation with various condiments and the deep rich flavors that develop during the cooking are soul satisfying. The accompanying condiments are essential to the experience. When the rice is cooked in the bean broth, it becomes black, although you could also cook plain white rice to go with this. A variation of the dish using *X-pelon* or *espelon*, similar to black-eyed peas, is also fairly common and black-eyed peas work well for that. Do not be intimidated by the large yield of the recipe if you do not have as many guests; you will want leftovers and they freeze well.

Serves 8 to 10

1. Salt and pepper the meat. Mix the recado and the juice or vinegar together, then mix in with the pork to marinate.

2. Bring the beans and the water to boil in a large pot and cook for 1 hour.

3. Brown the pork in 1/2 of the lard.

4. Add 1/2 of the white onion, the garlic, epazote, chile and the meat and bones to the beans. Cook for 1-1/2 hours on slow boil.

5. Remove the chile and the bones and discard. Reserve 2-1/4 cups of the broth for the rice.

6. Taste for salt and simmer for 30 minutes more (the beans should become soft and fork tender).

7. Sauté the rice and the remaining onion in 2 tablespoons lard until the rice begins to show color. Add the tomatoes, salt and reserved bean broth.

(continued on page 136)

Salt and pepper, to taste

2-1/2 to 3 pounds pork butt, leg, country ribs or stew meat, cut in 2-inch cubes

2 tablespoons Recado Colorado (see recipe on page 29)

2 tablespoons sour orange juice or mild fruity vinegar

1 pound dried black beans, sorted and washed

2 quarts water

2 + 2 tablespoons pork lard or vegetable oil

2 medium white onions, diced, divided

12 cloves garlic, toasted and peeled

4 to 5 sprigs epazote or 3 tablespoons dried epazote

1 habanero chile, charred and left whole (optional)

Pork bones for flavor (optional)

1 cup rice

1 tomato, chopped

1/2 teaspoon salt

1 batch Chiltomate (see recipe on page 44), warmed

Garnishes:

Radishes, sliced

Cilantro, chopped

Limes, sliced

Red onion, chopped

Chopped green cabbage

Hot green chiles, toasted, peeled, seeded and diced, or Chile Tumulado (see recipe on page 49)

Avocado, sliced or diced

Warm corn tortillas

Bring to a boil, stir well, cover and reduce to simmer. Cook for 25 minutes, remove from the heat and let sit (with the cover still on) for 20 minutes more.

8. Serve the pork and beans next to the rice, top with some of the Chiltomate and serve the garnishes alongside.

Cuban-Style Roasted Pork

A SIMPLER VERSION OF PIT-ROASTED PORK than Cochinita Pibil, Lechón Horneado illustrates the influence of Cuba on the cooking of the Yucatán peninsula. It makes a tasty main dish or the meat may be shredded to serve in tacos with an array of salsas and condiments.

Serves 6 to 8 as a main dish or 10 to 12 for tacos

1. Make small slices through the fat all over the surface of the pork.

2. Combine the juice, recado, garlic, salt and hot sauce and rub over the surface of the meat, working it into the slits.

3. Marinate the meat for at least 2 hours or overnight.

4. Toast the banana leaf to make it flexible (see page 19). Wrap the pork in the banana leaf and place in a baking dish OR place in a baking dish and cover with foil.

5. Bake at 375 degrees F for 2 hours, uncover and cook for 45 minutes more.

6. Cut in serving-sized pieces or shred for tacos.

---

1 pork leg or shoulder (3 to 4 pounds)

1-1/4 cups sour orange juice OR 1 cup fresh orange juice with 2 tablespoons mild vinegar or lime juice added

1-1/2 tablespoons Recado de Bistec (see recipe on page 31)

4 cloves garlic, roasted, peeled and mashed

1-1/2 teaspoons salt

1 to 2 tablespoons bottled habanero hot sauce (optional)

1 large banana leaf or heavy-duty foil

Albóndigas con Yerba Buena
Minted Meatballs

1/3 cup fresh mint leaves

1 tablespoon raisins

1 tablespoon toasted almonds

2 teaspoons capers

1-1/2 pounds ground beef, pork
or a mix

1 tablespoon Xac or Salpimentado
recados (see recipes on pages 36
and 33)

1 teaspoon salt

1 egg, well beaten

2 tablespoons masa harina or
bread crumbs

4 tablespoons vegetable oil, divided

1 recipe Chiltomate (see recipe on
page 44)

1 cup broth or water

1 (8-ounce) package fideos or thin
vermicelli broken into 1-inch
pieces (optional)

THIS IS A HOMESTYLE DISH that can also be found in small restaurants
serving *comida corrida* (inexpensive lunch). When made with the fideos,
it is a Yucatán version of spaghetti and meatballs. Prepared without the
pasta, it may serve as an appetizer or over rice as a main dish.

Serves 4 to 6

1. Chop the mint leaves, raisins, almonds and capers and mix with the meat
   in a bowl. Mix in the recado and salt, then the egg and finally the masa
   harina.

2. Let the mixture sit for 15 to 20 minutes, then form into large meatballs
   (about 12 to 18 total).

3. Brown the meatballs in 1/2 of the oil, add the Chiltomate and broth or
   water and simmer for 15 to 20 minutes.

4. Meanwhile, in a separate pan, sauté the fideos in the remaining oil until
   golden brown, then add to the meatball pan. Cook for about 15 minutes
   until the pasta is al dente and serve.

Lebanese Meat and Cracked Wheat Patties

WHAT IS MIDDLE EASTERN FOOD doing in Maya cooking? Several places in Mexico have significant populations of Lebanese immigrants, most notably the Yucatán peninsula. The Maya people have readily adapted many foreign influences and the "kibbeh" is one that is widely popular. Also often made with fish or no meat at all for lent, these Kibes are in the style of the street vendors in Chetumal, Quintana Roo. They can be served along with any good sauce or salsa; my favorite accompaniment is sliced cucumbers, Cebollas Moradas Encurtidas (see recipe on page 99) and Xnipec salsa (see recipe on page 40).

Serves 4 to 6 as a main course

1. At least 1 hour in advance, boil 4 cups of water and pour over the wheat. When the liquid has cooled to room temperature, drain and then squeeze out any excess water.

2. Mix all of the ingredients, except the oil, well and let sit for 15 minutes for the flavors to blend.

3. Divide the mixture into 12 equal parts. Form into "torpedoes" (football-shaped).

4. Heat the oil and fry the Kibes at 350 degrees F until well browned and cooked through. Drain and serve.

3/4 pound bulgur or cracked wheat

1 pound ground beef or turkey

1/2 cup finely minced green onions or scallions

1/3 cup mild green chiles (Anaheim, poblano, New Mexican), diced very fine

1/4 chile habanero, smashed to liquefy or 1 to 2 teaspoons bottled habanero sauce

1/2 cup mint or cilantro leaves (or a mix), finely chopped

1-1/2 teaspoons salt

1 teaspoon ground black pepper

1/2 teaspoon toasted and ground cumin seed

1/2 cup sliced almonds or piñon nuts, lightly toasted (optional)

Vegetable oil for frying

Butifarras Yucatecas
Yucatán Breakfast Sausages

1-3/4 pounds ground pork

1/2 pound ground beef (optional, you may use all pork)

1-1/2 tablespoons Escabeche, Salpimentado or de Bistec reca-dos (see recipes on pages 32, 33 and 31)

2 teaspoons anise seed, lightly toast-ed and ground

1-1/2 teaspoons salt

4 eggs, well beaten

Sausage casings or foil

THESE TASTY SAUSAGES ARE NOT STRICTLY for breakfast; we used to serve them regularly for brunch when I was the chef at the Coyote Cafe, and I know them by that name. Although they are wonderful with eggs or French toast for breakfast, they are more typically served in the Yucatán as a snack or antojito along with Cebollas Moradas Encurtidas (see recipe on page 99), slices of cheese and crusty bread or tortillas all washed down with icy cerveza. This recipe makes quite a few sausages; however, they freeze well after steaming.

Serves 8 to 10

1. Mix all of the ingredients thoroughly and stuff into the sausage casing in 4-inch links or wrap 1-inch-thick by 4-inch-long cylinders in foil.

2. Steam for 30 minutes until cooked through.

3. Cool completely; unwrap if using foil.

4. Cook over charcoal or in an oiled sauté pan until nicely browned.

Rellenos de Repollo
Stuffed Cabbage Fritters

For the Filling

2 tablespoons vegetable oil

1/2 cup diced onion

3 cloves garlic, minced

1 pound pork, chicken or turkey, seasoned, cooked (boiled or roasted) and then shredded NOTE: Leftover meats work well here and you may also use ground pork, beef or turkey

2 medium tomatoes, charred, skinned and chopped

2 teaspoons Recado de Bistec (see recipe on page 31) OR 1/2 teaspoon each ground canela, ground allspice, Mexican oregano and 1/4 teaspoon ground cloves

Salt and pepper, to taste

12 pimento-stuffed green olives, chopped

1/3 cup raisins

RELLENOS ARE NOT ALWAYS CHILES. In Spanish, the verb *rellenar* means to stuff, so anything that contains a filling is a relleno. These crunchy little packages of cabbage filled with meat are a scrumptious treat and also a good way to use leftover meats. In Chiapas where they originate, the rellenos are usually prepared using green cabbage; however, using red or purple cabbage makes for a dramatic presentation.

Serves 6

1. To make the filling, heat 2 tablespoons vegetable oil in a pan and cook the onion and garlic until beginning to brown. Add the meat and cook for 2 minutes, then add the tomatoes and fry for 2 minutes more. Add the seasonings, olives and raisins, stir well and remove from the heat.

2. Blanch the cabbage leaves, 1 at a time for about 30 seconds in boiling, salted water and immediately plunge them into very cold water to stop the cooking. Drain well and pat dry.

3. Divide the picadillo (filling) between the 12 cabbage leaves and wrap each one completely in the leaf to make a sealed package. Place in the refrigerator to firm the rellenos.

4. To make the salsa, heat 2 tablespoons oil in a tall-sided heavy pan or skillet and fry the strained Chiltomate for about 2 minutes while stirring. Add the masa harina to the broth and mix until smooth, then add to the salsa along with the seasonings. Simmer for about 10 minutes or until it is as thick as you like. Keep warm for serving.

5. Beat the egg whites with the salt until medium peaks have formed. Mix the flour with the yolks until smooth and fold into the egg whites.

6. Heat the oil for frying between 350 and 360 degrees F. Dip each relleno in the egg and flour batter and fry in the oil until golden brown on all sides. Drain well and serve with some of the salsa and a sprinkle of cheese.

For the Rellenos

12 outer leaves from a medium red or green cabbage that has been cored and halved

4 eggs, separated

1/2 teaspoon salt

1-1/2 tablespoons flour

Vegetable oil for frying

For the Salsa

2 tablespoons vegetable oil

1 recipe Chiltomate (see recipe on page 44), puréed smooth and strained

1 tablespoon masa harina

1 cup broth from cooking the meat for the filling, chicken broth or water (cool)

Generous pinch ground cloves

1/2 teaspoon ground canela

Salt and pepper, to taste

Poultry

THE MAYA HAVE USED MANY BIRDS for sustenance since pre-Hispanic days. They hunted the abundant wild fowl and there is evidence of domestication of turkeys and some smaller birds like doves. The Spanish introduced the chicken and modern methods of raising food animals to reinforce this practice. The city and village markets are full of chickens and turkeys and almost all rural families raise their own. The following recipes will show you some of the ways that poultry is prepared in Maya culture, from simple everyday dishes to elaborate feast-day masterpieces.

Pollo en Escabeche Valladolid
Seasoned and Grilled Chicken with Aromatic Sauce

1-1/2 quarts chicken broth or water

2 teaspoons salt

8 bone-in chicken quarters

3 tablespoons olive or vegetable oil

1 large white onion, peeled and
  diced

1/2 cup diced sweet red or yellow
  bell pepper

1/2 cup finely diced tomatoes

3 to 4 xcatic, guero or yellow hot
  chiles, roasted and left whole

1 or 2 habanero chiles, roasted and
  left whole (optional)

1 red onion, peeled, quartered and
  roasted

8 to 10 cloves garlic, roasted and
  peeled

1 sprig fresh thyme or marjoram
  OR 1 tablespoon toasted
  Mexican oregano

5 to 6 mint leaves OR 3 sprigs fresh
  cilantro

4 bay leaves, toasted

6 whole cloves (1/2 teaspoon),
  ground

VALLADOLID, IN THE HEART OF THE YUCATÁN PENINSULA, is a city with a colorful history. Today, the autopista (superhighway) between Cancun and Merida bypasses it by a few miles so most tourists do not stop, allowing Valladolid to maintain its traditions and tranquility. It is known throughout the peninsula as a place of great cooking; the food there is often a mix of Maya ingredients influenced by a Spanish heritage. *Escabeche* is a term in Spanish for sousing that means marinated, pickled or cooked in a vinegary liquid. This recipe makes for great leftovers so it is worth cooking more than you can use at one meal. Everything up to the grilling of the chicken may be accomplished ahead of time and refrigerated until ready to use.

Serves 8

1. Place the broth or water and the salt in a large saucepan or pot and heat to boiling. Add the chicken pieces. Return to a boil, then reduce the heat and simmer.

2. Preheat a skillet, add the oil and brown the diced white onion and sweet peppers. Add the tomatoes and fry for 1 more minute.

3. Add this mixture to the chicken pot along with the chiles, red onion, garlic, herbs, cloves and pepper. Simmer until the chicken is just cooked through, 20 to 25 minutes.

4. Remove the chicken to cool.

5. Cook the broth at a low boil for about 10 to 15 more minutes to thicken a little.

6. Mix 1/2 of the orange juice mix with the recado and rub over all of the surface of the chicken.

7. Char-grill, oven broil or bake the chicken in a 400-degree oven until golden brown.

8. Mix the remaining orange juice mix with the broth and ladle over the chicken to serve.

6 whole peppercorns (1/2 teaspoon), ground

3/4 cup sour orange juice OR 1/2 cup sweet orange juice with 1/4 cup mild, fruity vinegar (pineapple, apple cider or unseasoned rice vinegar is best)

3 tablespoons Recado Escabeche or Recado de Bistec (see recipes on pages 32 and 31)

 *Pollo Pibil*

Pit-Roasted Chicken with Yucatán Spices

2 fryer-sized chickens, 1 or 2 roaster sized chickens or 1 small turkey, whole or cut into serving pieces

4 tablespoons Recado Colorado (see recipe on page 29)

12 cloves garlic, peeled

1 medium white onion, coarsely chopped (3/4 cup)

2 tablespoons whole allspice berries, toasted and cracked OR 1 tablespoon ground allspice

2 tablespoons Mexican oregano, toasted

1 teaspoon cumin seed, toasted and crushed

2 teaspoons cracked black pepper

6 bay leaves, toasted

2 tablespoons Worcestershire sauce (optional—not traditional, but I did learn the trick in Mexico)

3/4 cup sour orange juice OR 1/2 cup sweet orange juice plus 1 tablespoon mild, fruity vinegar

1/4 cup mild, fruity vinegar

2 to 3 fresh habanero or Scotch bonnet chiles, stems and seeds removed, OR 2 to 3 tablespoons bottled habanero chile sauce

THIS IS THE CHICKEN VERSION of Cochinita Pibil and it is more common in contemporary Maya regional restaurants than the pork dish. The recipe works equally well with turkey, and that bird was almost certainly used in its pre-Columbian incarnation. I have had equally good results with both. Pollo Pibil may be prepared with the whole chicken or turkey; however, I buy large and use cut-up parts and package it in individual servings. This method simplifies the process, especially when it comes time to serve. This recipe may be easily halved for cooking one chicken.

Serves 8 to 10 as a main courses or enough for 42 to 48 tacos

1. Rinse, pat dry and then place the chicken in a freezer bag or other large plastic bag or a large nonreactive container.

2. Puree all the ingredients except the epazote, sliced onions, tomatoes and the banana leaves in a blender. Pour the marinade in with the chicken, seal bag and distribute well to coat. Marinate at least 2 hours or overnight in the refrigerator.

3. Preheat oven to 325 degrees F.

4. Toast the banana leaves to make them more pliable. Lay them out in pieces large enough to fully wrap each portion.

5. Remove the chicken from the bag and reserve the marinade.

6. Place each portion on a banana leaf. Pour about 1 tablespoon of the marinade over top of the chicken, then add an epazote leaf and some onion and tomato slices (if using this option).

7. Fold the leaf around the chicken to make a sealed package. Tie strips of banana leaves around this package from both directions to secure. NOTE: See Cochinita Pibil (page 126) for instructions on how to wrap a whole bird.

8. Bake at 325 degrees F for 1-1/4 to 1-3/4 hours (2-1/2 to 3 hours, depending on size, for a whole turkey), until the meat is 185 degrees F and fork tender. Leaves will be slightly darkened on the outside when finished.

9. Allow to cool for 10 minutes; slit open banana leaves with a sharp knife or scissors (be careful of the steam) and remove the chicken or present on the leaves.

Condiment suggestions: Fresh Corn Tortillas (see recipe on page 72), chopped cilantro, citrus wedges, Xnipek salsa (see recipe on page 40), Cebollas Moradas Encurtidas (see recipe on page 99), Salpicón de Rábanos (see recipe on page 48), Guacamole (see recipe on page 57), Rice and Beans or Frijoles Negros de Olla (see recipes on pages 104 and 94) and Xol-Chon Kek (see recipe on page 90).

2 tablespoons vegetable oil

2 tablespoons salt

Leaves from several epazote sprigs (optional)

Thin slices of 2 red onions (optional)

3 to 4 medium tomatoes, sliced (optional)

1 (1-pound) package frozen banana leaves (available at specialty food stores and Latin American or Asian grocers). Thaw and rinse well in cool water. Tear 8 half-inch-wide strips off 1 leaf and tie 2 together to make 4 strips to use later for ties OR use heavy-duty aluminum foil

Pollo en Pipian Rojo
Chicken in Red Chile-Pumpkinseed Sauce

PUMPKINSEEDS WERE VITAL TO pre-Hispanic Maya people and still play an important role in the cuisine today. The seeds of pumpkin and squash are prized even more than the flesh of theses plants, as the seeds provide protein and much needed fats for energy. Sauces thickened with seeds are called pipíans and they are the precursors of moles, which utilize a blend of indigenous and old-world ingredients. This recipe uses chicken, common in contemporary times, although in the past this recipe would have been just as likely to use pheasant, quail, armadillo or venison and can be adapted to work with all of the above. To mimic the flavor of *pibil* cooking, I like to finish the chicken on the grill before combining it with the sauce, but you may also cook it through in the pot or oven to omit that step.

Serves 4 to 6

1. Place the chicken in a pot with the cool water, recado and salt. Slowly bring to a boil and reduce to simmer. Cook for 45 minutes, occasionally skim off any foam or scum that rises to the surface. Remove chicken from the cooking liquid.

2. Place the chiles, tomatoes, onion, garlic, recado and spices in a blender and puree smooth.

3. Heat the oil in a tall-sided, heavy pot and strain the puree into it. Fry for 2 to 3 minutes while stirring until the color deepens.

4. Add the pumpkinseeds and slowly add most of the broth while stirring to make a smooth sauce. Adjust for salt and simmer for 10 minutes, adding more liquid as needed; keep warm.

5. Cook the chicken on a preheated char-grill until nicely browned.

6. Lay the chicken pieces in the pipían and serve.

1 fryer chicken, 3 to 4 pounds, cut into serving pieces

Cool water to cover

1 tablespoon Recado Colorado or Recado de Bistec (see recipes on pages 29 and 31)

1-1/2 teaspoons salt

2 or 3 chiles secos Yucatecos or other hot red chiles and 2 ancho chiles, toasted, stemmed, seeded and soaked, then drained (see page 24)

3 small to medium tomatoes, charred

1 medium onion, peeled, sliced in thirds and pan-toasted

6 cloves garlic, pan-toasted and peeled

1 teaspoon Recado Colorado (see recipe on page 29) or ground annatto seeds

1 teaspoon toasted, ground allspice

1/2 teaspoon ground canela

1/4 teaspoon ground black pepper

2 tablespoons vegetable oil or lard

1 cup pumpkinseeds, well toasted and finely ground

2 to 2-1/2 cups chicken broth or water (or use the broth from cooking the chicken and then omit the 1 teaspoon of Recado Colorado)

Salt, to taste

Pavo Almendrado
Turkey in Almond Sauce

3 to 4 xcatic, guero, yellow hot or
    hot green chiles, roasted,
    stemmed, seeded and peeled,
    divided

1 cup sliced almonds, lightly
    toasted, divided

1 tablespoon Recado de Bistec (see
    recipe on page 31)

1 large or 2 medium onions, peeled,
    sliced in thirds and pan-roasted

10 cloves garlic, roasted and peeled

1 small to medium tomato, charred

1/2 cup green pitted olives

1 tablespoon mild, fruity vinegar

1 small slice of white bread, pan-
    toasted golden brown in olive oil
    OR 2 tablespoons bread crumbs

3 cups turkey or chicken broth or
    water, divided

1/4 cup olive oil

Salt and pepper, to taste

2 to 2-1/2 pounds turkey tenderloin
    or thighs (use 20 percent more
    weight if the turkey still has
    bones)

Chopped cilantro or parsley to
    garnish

MANY RECIPES USED IN THIS REGION retain their Mediterranean influences. In this one the old-world ingredients, almonds, onions and olives, are combined with native herbs, chiles and the favorite Maya protein, turkey, although you could certainly substitute chicken. Serve with fried plantain slices or boiled, sliced chayote, and Arroz Amarillo (see recipe on page 98).

Serves 6

1. Dice half of the chiles and reserve. Reserve 1/4 cup of the toasted almonds for garnish and grind the rest to a fine powder.

2. Puree the recado, remaining chiles, onions, garlic, tomato, olives, vinegar, toasted bread and 1/2 cup of the broth smooth in a blender.

3. Heat the olive oil in a heavy skillet or Dutch oven, salt and pepper the turkey and brown in the oil on all sides. Remove from the oil and set aside.

4. Fry the puree in the oil for 2 to 3 minutes while stirring. Add the ground almonds and enough broth to make a thin sauce. Bring to a slow boil and add the browned turkey.

5. Reduce the heat and simmer until the turkey is cooked through (20 to 25 minutes, more for bone-in), adding broth or water as needed to prevent burning due to over-thickening.

6. Remove the turkey and slice. Cover each portion with a generous amount of sauce and garnish with the diced chiles, toasted almonds and chopped cilantro.

Char-Grilled Turkey

TURKEY IS AN IMPORTANT FOOD throughout the Maya world. In pre-Columbian times, it was hunted and eventually became domesticated. Some restaurants have replaced it with chicken, which is considered more upscale; however, the flavor of turkey is, in my opinion, richer and more satisfying, although chicken is a fine substitute. The original recipe was designed to prepare a whole turkey of 12 to 14 pounds, but I have chosen to use smaller parts of a turkey here to make it easier for the home cook. If you would like to cook a whole turkey this way for a special occasion, just double the quantities of the recado and the escabeche and proceed.

This method of preparation is great for a special meal and the resulting leftovers are perfect for many other Maya-influenced dishes like Panuchos, Salbutes, sincronizados, soups, salpicón, and tortas. Although the recipe calls for boiling the turkey before grilling it, leftover roast turkey may also be seasoned with the recado and grilled to duplicate the enchanting flavor that this recipe creates.

Serves 6 to 8

For the Turkey

1. Place the turkey in a large cooking pot, add all of the remaining seasonings and enough water to cover.

2. Bring to a boil, cook for 15 minutes, reduce to simmer and skim off any foam that is formed.

3. Return to a low boil and cook until the turkey is cooked through completely (about 1 hour 20 minutes).

4. Remove the turkey and strain the broth (the remaining broth makes a good soup base).

(continued on page 156)

For the Turkey

1 large turkey breast (bone-in) OR several turkey leg and thigh quarters OR 1 whole roasting/stewing chicken (5 to 7 pounds total)

6 bay leaves, toasted

4 to 5 sprigs fresh oregano or marjoram

3 to 4 sprigs fresh thyme or 1 tablespoon dried thyme

1 onion, quartered

1 roasted garlic head, cut in half across

10 whole peppercorns, toasted

6 whole allspice berries, toasted

1 tablespoon salt

Water to cover the turkey

For the Recado

4 ounces Recado Colorado (see recipe on page 29) using all of the options

NOTE: You could also use commercially prepared achiote paste and add all of the options for the recado along with the addition here

1 tablespoon ground canela

Generous pinch saffron (optional)

1 teaspoon salt

1/3 cup sour orange juice OR 1/4 cup sweet orange juice plus 2 tablespoons apple cider or other mild, fruity vinegar

For the Escabeche

3/4 cup olive oil

2 white onions, sliced

12 cloves garlic, roasted and peeled

4 to 5 xcatic, Guero (yellow hot) or New Mexican green chiles, roasted, peeled, seeded and stemmed, then cut into strips

12 whole black peppercorns

6 whole allspice berries, toasted

2 teaspoons salt

4 bay leaves, toasted

2 inches canela stick

4 whole cloves

1 tablespoon Mexican oregano, toasted

1/2 teaspoon cumin seed, toasted

2 cups sour orange juice OR 1-3/4 cups sweet orange juice plus 1/4 cup mild, fruity vinegar or lime juice

1-1/2 cups of the cooking liquid for the turkey, strained (if using roast turkey here, add turkey or chicken broth instead)

For the Recado

1. Combine all of the recado ingredients into a paste and rub it over the surface of the turkey (inside and out).

2. Allow to marinate for at least 30 minutes.

3. Char-grill (preferably over wood or charcoal), turning occasionally to prevent burning, until the surface is all caramelized and there are some blackened edges (about 25 minutes).

4. Allow to cool and then slice into portions or shred for other recipes.

5. Serve with the escabeche alongside.

For the Escabeche

1. Heat the oil in a heavy pan and sauté the onions until transparent. Add the garlic and the chiles, then the spices. Add the liquid and bring to a boil.

2. Remove from the heat and allow to cool completely and sit for at least 2 hours to develop flavor.

3. Strain and serve or store in the refrigerator.

Pollo Alcaparrado
Chicken in Caper Sauce

THIS DISH, WHICH IS A BLEND of Maya and Spanish influences, is from the state of Campeche and is very easy to prepare if you already have the recado on hand. The elements of the sauce may be pureed for a more refined look or left intact for a rustic look. Traditionally made using bone-in chicken parts, but boneless breast, pork loin chops or tenderloin slices may also be used. Alcaparrado dishes are usually served with rice and garnished with parsley or cilantro and Cebollas Moradas Encurtidas (see recipe on page 99).

Serves 4 to 6

1. Combine the recado and the juice, and marinate the chicken in half of this mixture for at least one hour and up to overnight.

2. In a heavy skillet or casserole dish, heat the oil and sauté the sweet pepper for a few minutes. Add the onion and the tomatoes and fry 2 to 3 minutes more.

3. Add the raisins, capers, olives, roasted garlic, chiles and the remaining juice and recado mixture. Season with salt and pepper, and simmer for 5 to 7 minutes, adding a little water or chicken broth as needed to keep the sauce moist. Puree, if desired (leave the chiles intact), and return to the pan.

NOTE: *If you puree the sauce, you may want to reserve some of the capers, olives and raisins or use extra for garnish.*

4. Char-grill or sauté the chicken until done.

5. Place the cooked chicken in the sauce and warm together for a few minutes to combine the flavors.

---

1 tablespoon Recado de Alcaparrado OR Recado de Bistec (see recipes on pages 37 and 31)

3/4 cup sour orange juice OR 1/2 cup sweet orange juice + 2 tablespoons mild, fruity vinegar

1 whole fryer chicken (3 to 3-1/2 pounds), cut into serving-sized pieces or your choice of chicken or pork cuts

2 tablespoons olive or vegetable oil

1 sweet red or green pepper, diced (optional)

1 medium white onion, peeled, sliced, pan-roasted and diced

3/4 cup diced tomato

1/8 cup raisins (optional)

1/4 cup capers, drained

12 pimento-stuffed green olives, sliced

12 cloves garlic, pan-toasted, peeled and sliced in half lengthwise

2 xcatic, guero or yellow hot chiles OR 1 habanero chile, charred and left whole

Salt and pepper, to taste

Pavo en Relleno Negro
Turkey in Black Sauce with Stuffed Pork Roll

For the Turkey

1 small (10 to 13 pound) turkey or 2 large chickens

2 teaspoons salt

1 recipe (1 pounds) Chilmole o Recado de Relleno Negro (see recipe on page 30), mixed with 1 cup warm water and strained NOTE: Reserve 1 tablespoon for the pork

1 teaspoon cumin seeds, toasted and ground

12 cloves garlic, roasted until mostly blackened and peeled

2 sprigs fresh epazote, 1 tablespoon dried epazote OR 2 teaspoons toasted Mexican oregano

1 large or 2 small white onions, quartered and pan-roasted, then peeled and cut into strips

2 medium tomatoes (about 8 ounces), quickly charred and cut into strips

1 red or green sweet pepper, slightly charred, stemmed, seeded and sliced in strips

2 xcatic, yellow hot or jalapeño chiles, charred and left whole

2 tablespoons flour or 4 tablespoons masa harina

Water as needed

COUNTLESS YUCATECO RESTAURANTS around the peninsula feature this turkey preparation, unusual for North Americans as the turkey is simmered rather than roasted and the shiny black sauce is distinctively eye-catching. Variations abound and it is also served in the Maya populated states of Campeche, Quintana Roo and parts of Tabasco. Intended for special occasions and usually put together to feed many guests, Relleno Negro can be made with chicken instead of turkey and the "relleno," or stuffed pork may be omitted to keep it simple.

Serves 10 to 16 depending on the size of the bird

For the Turkey

1. Cut the turkey into serving-sized pieces.

2. Place turkey in a pot; add enough water to cover along with the salt, recado, cumin, garlic and epazote. Mix well, bring to a boil, reduce the heat to simmer, cover and cook for 1 to 1-1/2 hours, until the turkey is getting tender. NOTE: Chicken will take less time.

3. Add the onion, tomato strips and pepper strips along with the whole chiles, simmer for 30 minutes longer (add the pork roll at this time if cooking this method).

4. Mix the flour or masa harina with some cool water to make a thin paste and add it to the broth. Stir well and cook about 10 more minutes to thicken.

For the Pork Roll (Relleno)

1. Heat the oil in a saucepan and sauté the onions, peppers and garlic for 2 minutes, add the pork and cook for 2 to 3 minutes more (DO NOT over-cook).

2. Remove to a mixing bowl and cool. Mix in the raw eggs, masa or bread crumbs, recado and season with salt and pepper.

For the Pork Roll (Relleno)

2 tablespoons vegetable oil or lard

1/2 cup diced white onion

1/2 cup diced red, green or mixed, sweet pepper

1 clove garlic, minced

1-1/2 pounds ground pork

2 raw eggs

2 tablespoons masa harina or bread crumbs

1 tablespoon Chilmole o Recado de Relleno Negro (reserved from recipe for turkey above) dissolved in 1 tablespoon mild vinegar

Salt and pepper, to taste

Cheesecloth and twine

4 to 6 epazote leaves, 2 tablespoons mint leaves or 3 tablespoons fresh oregano or marjoram leaves, finely chopped

6 hard-boiled eggs, peeled

3. Lay out several layers of cheesecloth to form a rectangle about 12x24 inches.

4. Spread the meat mixture to form a rectangle measuring 7x14 inches, sprinkle with the epazote and lay the hard-boiled eggs down the center.

5. Wrap the cheesecloth around the pork to form a cylinder with the eggs in the center. Secure with twine or string.

6. Place in the pot with the turkey and cook during the last 30 minutes of the turkey. NOTE: You may also cook this separately with turkey or chicken broth.

7. Remove from the pan, cool slightly and cut away the cheesecloth.

8. Slice across to reveal the egg stuffing and serve with pieces of the cooked turkey.

9. Pavo en Relleno Negro is usually served with rice or tamales.

Turkey in Black Seasoning Paste

THIS IS THE CAMPECHANA STYLE OF COOKING turkey in the stunning black sauce called chilmole. It is much less complicated than the similar Pavo en Relleno Negro, yet retains all of the exotic qualities. In Campeche, just about any type of meat is prepared in this fashion: turkey, chicken, pork, beef and venison. Prepared in advance and reheated to serve, the flavors are even richer. Serve with white rice for a striking contrast of colors.

Serves 6 to 8

1. Salt and pepper and cook the turkey about 2/3 of the way done, either on a char-grill, in the oven or by boiling in water seasoned with 2 garlic cloves, 6 peppercorns, 4 whole allspice berries, 1-1/2 teaspoons salt and a sprig of fresh epazote or several bay leaves (optional).

2. Mix the masa harina with 1-1/2 cups of the broth and dissolve until smooth.

3. Mix the recado with the remaining broth, add the masa mixture and stir until smooth. Add the tomatoes, onion and the turkey and bring to a boil.

4. Reduce the heat, cover and simmer, stirring occasionally and adding broth as needed to prevent burning, for 30 to 40 minutes or until the turkey is tender.

5. Serve the turkey in the chilmole garnished with the chopped eggs.

Salt and pepper, to taste

About 5 pounds turkey legs or thighs

1/2 cup masa harina or 1 cup fresh masa

6 cups turkey or chicken broth or water (if you boil the turkey, use the strained broth from that), divided

1/2 recipe (8 ounces) Chilmole o Recado de Relleno Negro (see recipe on page 30)

2 to 3 medium tomatoes, cut in eighths (wedges)

1 medium white onion, peeled and cut into 1/4-inch-thick strips

3 to 4 hard-boiled eggs, peeled and chopped, for garnish

Seafood

FROM THE GULF COAST ON THE WEST, north around the Yucatán Peninsula and south along the Caribbean coast, the Maya have made use of the abundant seafood that they harvested from these bountiful waters since before recorded history. *Jaiba* (crab), *almejas* (clams), *caracol* (conch), *langosta* (lobster), *ostiones* (oysters) and *camaron* (shrimp) are the common shellfish used in the cooking of this region. Fish species found here include, *huachinango* (red snapper), *mero* (grouper), *robalo* (snook), *pargo* (snapper), *sierra* (mackerel), *Dorado* (mahimahi), *mojarra* (perch), *pámpano* (pompano), *atún* (tuna), *cornoado* (amberjack), *sábalo* (tarpon), *cazón* (baby shark or dogfish), *tiburón* (shark) and *rubia* (yellowtail), along with *pulpo* (octopus) and *calamar* (squid).

Traditional dishes like ceviche, pescado frito, tikin xic, mac cum and filete rellenos are served in the many seaside palapa restaurants and in villages and homes along the coast with contemporary variations and optional creations presented at resort restaurants and in the colonial cities of Merida and Campeche. The recipes listed here may also be successfully prepared using other seafood varieties from the oceans of the world. The most important criteria for seafood from the Maya regions is freshness.

Pescado en Escabeche
Fish in Aromatic Sauce

2 to 3 pounds fresh fish filets, cut into 2-inch-wide pieces

3 tablespoons lime juice

Salt and pepper to season the filets

1/3 cup olive or vegetable oil

2 large red or white onions, peeled and sliced

1 carrot, peeled and sliced (optional)

4 cloves garlic, roasted, then peeled

3 to 4 chiles and/or sweet peppers such as xcatic, yellow hot, habanero, Anaheim, poblano or sweet red, green or yellow peppers, roasted, seeded, peeled and cut into large pieces or strips. NOTE: You can use one variety or a mix. Often the smaller chiles are left intact without peeling or seeding

3 to 4 bay leaves, toasted

3 tablespoons Recado de Escabeche (see recipe on page 32)

2 (1-inch-square) pieces orange zest

3/4 cup mild vinegar (apple cider, pineapple or rice work best)

1/4 cup water

Juice from 1 orange

1/2 cup diced tomatoes (optional)

LITERALLY PICKLED OR SOUSED FISH, Pescado en Escabeche is a Yucatán favorite. Variations abound but all generally contain onions, herbs and spices along with sweet peppers and/or mild chiles, all in a vinegary broth. Typically served as a main course, this preparation could be used for an appetizer and the fish makes an excellent filling for tacos. The fresher the fish, the better—and almost any type will do. I sometimes use this recipe to prepare large shrimp en escabeche too. It is also a useful method for preserving fresh fish that cannot be served for a day or two.

Serves 4 to 6 as a main course

1. Sprinkle the fish filets with the lime juice and salt and pepper. Set aside to marinate for 15 to 20 minutes.

2. Add the oil to a hot pan and cook the fish pieces on both sides until lightly browned.

3. Place the cooked fish in a heat-proof serving dish.

4. Return the pan to the heat and sauté the onions and carrot (if using) for about 2 minutes.

5. Add the garlic, chiles and/or peppers, bay leaves, Recado de Escabeche, orange zest, vinegar and water; bring to a boil, reduce the heat to a low boil and cook for 10 to 12 minutes. Add orange juice and the tomatoes (if using) and return to high heat to boil momentarily.

6. Pour the boiling escabeche over the fish filets, cover and let sit for 15 minutes.

7. To serve, remove the fish from the liquid and place in a serving dish. Reheat the liquid and vegetables and pour over the fish.

Pargo Adobado al Horno
Oven-Baked Porgy

THIS CAMPECHANO METHOD OF BAKING a whole seasoned fish, wrapped in banana leaves, produces a flavorful and moist result. Other species of whole fish or fish with good-sized filets, like snapper, sea bass, pompano, snook or even salmon, may be freely substituted. Most recipes for this method call for commercial recado adobo, available in many stores throughout the region. I have created a similar-tasting substitute for those of us not in Campeche, using one of the recados found in this book. If the fish is carefully wrapped in the leaves, you may also cook it on an outdoor grill.

Serves 6 to 8

1. Mix the Xak with the orange juice to make the adobo paste.

2. Rinse the fish in cold water and pat dry with paper towels.

3. Spread the adobo on all sides of the fish (including the body cavity for whole fish).

4. Toast the banana leaves to make them pliable (see page 19).

5. Place the banana leaf on a baking sheet or large roasting pan. NOTE: Use 1 large or several overlapping leaves to ensure a good seal that keeps the cooking juices around the fish.

6. Spread half of the tomatoes, onion, peppers and garlic on the banana leaf, approximately the size of the fish.

7. Lay the fish on top of the vegetables and spread the remaining vegetables on top. Sprinkle with the ancho chile powder and drizzle with olive oil. Wrap the banana leaf around to make a package and secure by tying strips of the banana leaf around the package.

8. Bake at 375 degrees F for approximately 40 minutes, until a knife or toothpick inserted into the package passes through the fish easily.

9. Open the top of the banana leaf package, spoon some of the collected juices over the fish and return to the oven for 10 to 12 minutes more to brown. Serve with rice, black beans and/or tamales.

2 tablespoons Xak (dry recado, see recipe on page 36)

3/4 cup sour orange juice OR 2/3 cup sweet orange juice and 2 tablespoons mild vinegar

1 whole porgy, other type of fish or fish filets, 3-1/2 to 4-1/2 pounds total

Banana leaves or foil for wrapping (enough to have a surface 3 to 4 times the size of the fish)

2 to 3 large tomatoes, cut in wedges

1 white onion, peeled and cut into 1/2-inch-thick strips or slices

1 sweet red, green or yellow pepper, seeded and sliced in 1/2-inch strips

2 cloves garlic, peeled and sliced

2 teaspoons ancho or other mild chile powder

3 to 4 tablespoons olive oil

Camarones Asados Yucatecos
Yucatán BBQ Shrimp

3/4 cup sour orange juice, 1/2 cup
  sweet orange juice with 2 tablespoons mild vinegar OR 2/3 cup
  lime juice and 1 tablespoon mild
  vinegar

3 tablespoons cool water

6 cloves garlic, toasted and peeled

1/2 to 1 habanero chile, charred
  and seeded OR 1 to 2 teaspoons
  habanero sauce (optional)

1 teaspoon salt

2 teaspoons vegetable oil

2 tablespoons Recado Colorado (see
  recipe on page 29) or achiote paste

1-1/2 tablespoons Recado Escabeche
  (see recipe on page 32) OR
  1 (1-1/2-inch) piece canela,
  6 whole cloves, 1/2 teaspoon
  toasted cumin seeds, 6 whole
  peppercorns; all ground AND
  1 medium white onion, peeled,
  sliced in 3 rounds and pan-
  roasted (see page 19)

1-1/2 to 2 pounds large shrimp, 21-
  25 size or larger (wild shrimp
  tastes much better than farm-
  raised), peeled (tail left on) and
  deveined

1/8 cup cilantro leaves, chopped, for
  garnish

IN MAYA COMMUNITIES AROUND THE Yucatán peninsula, meat and seafood cooked over hot coals is a much-loved repast. Whether you are visiting along the coast or in an interior village, the intoxicating smoke, redolent with achiote, citrus and habanero chiles, wafts through the air enticing you to seek out the source. This easy method for seasoning and grilling seafood is sure to satisfy you and your guests. Fresh fish, either cubed and placed on skewers or as whole filets, may be prepared in the same way.

Serves 4 to 6

1. Place everything except the shrimp and cilantro in a blender and process until smooth.

2. Toss the shrimp with the marinade, cover and refrigerate for 1 to 3 hours.

3. Place the shrimp on skewers and gently shake off any excess marinade.

4. Grill over hot coals, a gas grill or in a broiler until just done.

5. Garnish with the cilantro and serve.

Pan de Cazón
Stacked Tortillas with Shark

NO COOKBOOK ABOUT THIS REGION would be complete without Pan de Cazón, one of the most recognized seafood dishes from Campeche. The cooked cazón, a small shark or dogfish, is shredded and layered with black beans and corn tortillas, then topped with tomato sauce and avocado slices. Any firm whitefish, like halibut, sea bass, pompano, grouper, etc., that is suitable for shredding may be used and, although not traditional, I have successfully replaced the fish with shrimp or crab in this preparation.

Serves 4 to 6

For the Fish

1. Place all the ingredients except the fish in a pan with enough water to eventually cover the fish (about 3 to 4 cups).

2. Bring to a boil and cook for 10 minutes.

3. Add the fish, return to a boil, then reduce to simmer and cook for 12 to 15 more minutes, until the fish is cooked through.

4. Remove the fish and cool.

5. Shred the fish by hand using a fork, removing and skin and bones.

To Assemble

1. Heat the Chiltomate and the frijoles in separate pots.

2. Dip a tortilla in the tomato sauce and place on a plate. Spread the tortilla with a layer of beans, then some of the shredded shark. Repeat to make 4 layers per serving.

3. Top each stack with some of the remaining Chiltomate. Garnish with the avocado slices and serve immediately.

For the Fish

1 white onion, peeled and coarsely chopped

3 cloves garlic, peeled and coarsely chopped

3 to 4 bay leaves, toasted

1/2 teaspoon ground allspice, toasted

1/2 teaspoon black peppercorns, toasted

2 teaspoons Mexican oregano, toasted

1 orange, quartered with the peel on

1 teaspoon salt

1-1/2 pounds shark

Water to cover

To Assemble

Double recipe of Chiltomate (see recipe on page 44)

2-1/2 cups Frijoles Negros de Olla (see recipe on page 94)

16 to 20 corn tortillas

Sliced avocados for garnish

Pampano Pohchuc
Grilled Stuffed Pompano

1-3/4 to 2-1/2 pounds whole pompano, snapper, rockfish, etc., OR 1-1/2 to 2 pounds skin-on fish filets

Salt and pepper

2 tablespoons Xak (see recipe on page 36) OR Recado de Escabeche (see recipe on page 32)

3 tablespoons sour orange juice OR 2 tablespoons lime juice and 1 tablespoon mild, fruity vinegar

1/2 cup cubed potatoes

1/2 cup cubed carrots

4 tablespoons vegetable or olive oil, divided

1/4 cup diced onion

1 medium tomato, diced

1/2 cup fresh or frozen green peas

1/4 cup chopped cilantro or parsley

USING A STRAIGHTFORWARD APPROACH to cooking a whole fish on the grill, this pohchuc recipe comes from Campeche. In this method the whole fish is filled with vegetables, seasoned and then char-grilled, although many cooks add seafood to the filling as well. You may also bake the fish in the oven. While whole pompano is the fish called for, other types of whole fish or individual skin-on filets may also be used. If using the fish filets, simply make a slit in the fish, parallel to the skin to form a pocket, and place some of the filling inside.

Serves 4 to 6

1. Score the skin of the fish with parallel slits, 1/4 inch deep and 1/2 inch apart.

2. Salt and pepper the fish inside and out.

3. Mix the recado with the juice and rub on the outside of the fish, working some into each of the slits.

4. Cook the potato and carrot dices together in boiling salted water until cooked through, yet firm. Drain and cool.

5. Sauté the onion in 2 tablespoons of the oil for 2 minutes; add the potatoes and carrots and continue cooking for 2 to 3 more minutes.

6. Add the tomatoes, cook 1 minute more, remove from the heat and mix in the peas and cilantro. Stuff the fish with this mixture (you may want to secure the filling in the fish by weaving a wooden or bamboo skewer or several toothpicks to close the open side of the body cavity).

7. Gently brush the outside of the fish with the remaining 2 tablespoons of oil and char-grill about 4 minutes per side until the fish is cooked through, yet still moist. Serve with Budín de Chayote (see recipe on page 97), Yellow Rice (see recipe on page 98) and your favorite salsa.

Ensalada de Mariscos
Seafood Salad

ALONG THE WHITE SAND CARIBBEAN SHORELINE of the Riviera Maya in Quintana Roo, seafood is abundant and the residents and visitors enjoy it in many different preparations. This salad is a contemporary application of traditional flavors. The types of seafood that you may use are endless. Obviously, the fresher, the better. Try serving the salad in individual lettuce or cabbage leaves, crispy tortilla bowls or coconut shell halves.

Serves 4 to 6

1. Mix the recado with the juices, vinegar, chile, cilantro and 1/2 the zests and let sit for 5 minutes to develop flavor. Add salt and pepper and whisk in the olive oil.

2. Gently toss the dressing with the seafood, onion, cucumber and tomatoes.

3. Let sit for 15 to 30 minutes before serving to allow the flavors to mingle with the seafood.

4. Garnish with zest, lime wedges and Totopos or tortilla strips and serve.

1 tablespoon Recado de Especie o Mechado or Recado de Escabeche (see recipes on pages 33 and 32)

2 tablespoons lime juice

1 tablespoon sweet orange juice

1 teaspoon mild, fruity vinegar

1/2 habanero chile, charred, seeded and minced very fine (you may substitute other milder chiles, if preferred)

3 tablespoons chopped cilantro

1 teaspoon orange zest, minced fine (reserve 1/2 for garnish)

1 teaspoon lime zest, minced fine (reserve 1/2 for garnish)

Salt and pepper, to taste

3 tablespoons olive oil

1 to 1-1/2 pounds various cooked seafood (shrimp, fish, oysters, clams, squid, crab, lobster, etc.) in bite-sized pieces

1 medium red onion, sliced in thin strips and rinsed (see page 19)

1 small to medium cucumber, peeled, seeded, cut in half lengthwise and sliced across 1/4 inch thick

2 medium tomatoes, cut in 8 wedges

Lime wedges

Crispy tortilla strips or Totopos (see recipe on page 56)

173

Camarones al Coco Campechano
Coconut Shrimp

1-1/2 pounds shrimp 26-30 size or larger, peeled and deveined (tail left on)

2 tablespoons lime juice

Salt and pepper

1 teaspoon Xak (see recipe on page 36, optional)

2 eggs, well beaten

1-1/2 cups flour

Water as needed

1 cup cereal flakes (cornflakes, bran flakes, etc.), coarsely crushed

1-3/4 cups shredded, sweet coconut

Vegetable oil for frying

Sweet Sour and Hot Mango Sauce (recipe follows)

For the Mango Sauce

2 ripe mangos, peeled, seeded and diced

1 habanero chile (milder chiles may be used; however, the chile is left whole and does not add a lot of heat)

1 (2-inch) stick canela

3 to 4 whole cloves

1/3 cup sugar

1/4 cup water

2 teaspoons mild, fruity vinegar

MANY RESTAURANTS ALONG THE gulf shores of Campeche have built their reputations on this menu item. The crunchiness of the coconut-crusted shrimp matches well with the sweet, sour and slightly hot mango sauce. Other fruits like papaya, pineapple or apple may also be used. Camarones al Coco presents well as an appetizer, first course or main dish.

Serves 6 as a main course

1. Toss the shrimp with the lime juice, then season with the salt, pepper and Xak.

2. Mix the eggs with a dash of salt, then mix in the flour alternately with the water until all of the flour is incorporated and a smooth, thin, pancake-like batter is formed.

3. Combine the cereal flakes and coconut and dip the shrimp first in the batter, then roll in the coconut mixture.

4. Fry in 350- to 365-degree-F oil until golden brown. Drain and serve hot.

SWEET-AND-SOUR HOT MANGO SAUCE

1. Combine everything in a saucepan and cook on a slow boil until most of the liquid has evaporated.

2. Remove the chile, canela and cloves.

3. Serve chunky or puree smooth.

Chechac
Caribbean Coconut Fish Soup

I TASTED THIS SOUP, WITH A decidedly Belizean influence, in the area around Chetumal, Quintana Roo. The Maya word *chechac* implies a red-colored soup, which is achieved by using achiote in the coconut milk broth. Shellfish may also be added to this preparation. Serve alone as an early course or with white or yellow rice as a main dish.

Serves 6 to 8

1. Dissolve the recado in a little broth and place in a pot with the rest of the broth, coconut milk, vegetables, chile and thyme.

2. Bring to a slow boil and cook until the plantain is tender. Remove the chiles, chop and offer on the side.

3. Season the fish with the lime juice and salt and pepper and carefully lay them on the top of the soup. Cover the pot and simmer for about 15 minutes until the fish is cooked.

4. Remove the fish, stir in the cilantro, season with salt and pepper and ladle some of the soup in a bowl, then place the fish on top.

2 tablespoons Recado Colorado (see recipe on page 29)

1 quart fish or chicken broth or water

2 (13-ounce) cans coconut milk

1 white onion, peeled and cut into 1/2-inch-wide strips

2 sweet bell peppers, stemmed, seeded and cut into 1/2-inch-wide strips

1 large green plantain or 2 medium white potatoes, peeled and sliced

2 medium tomatoes, cut in wedges

1 or 2 habanero chiles, charred, stemmed, seeded and cut in two

2 sprigs fresh thyme or 2 teaspoons dried

2 to 2-1/2 pounds fish filet (skin-on works best to keep the fish from breaking up)

3 tablespoons lime juice

Salt and pepper, to taste

3 tablespoons chopped cilantro

Tikin-Xic
Mayan-Style Grilled Fish

*2/3 cup sour orange juice OR
1/2 cup sweet orange juice
with 2 tablespoons mild,
fruity vinegar*

2 tablespoons lime juice

*6 ounces Recado Colorado (see
recipe on page 29)*

*1 whole fish filet, 3 to 5 pounds,
skin on (snapper, sea bass,
grouper, pompano, mahimahi,
snook, etc.) or 8 to 10 individually
portioned filets*

Salt and pepper

*Several large banana leaves or
heavy-duty aluminum foil*

*1-1/2 tablespoons fresh oregano or
cilantro leaves*

3 to 4 medium tomatoes, sliced

*1 to 2 sweet red, green or yellow
peppers, cleaned and cut in
1-inch strips*

*1 large red onion, peeled and cut in
thin slices*

*2 or 3 xcatic, guero, yellow hot
or jalapeño chiles, charred and
split lengthwise OR 1 to 2 whole
habanero chiles, charred and
left intact*

*3 to 4 tablespoons olive or
vegetable oil*

THIS FLAVORFUL AND COLORFUL FISH RECIPE is prepared all along the coasts of the Yucatán, Campeche and Quintana Roo. The usual method is to score a whole skin-on filet of fish, season and wrap it in banana leaves with tomatoes, onions, sweet peppers and chiles and then char-grill the entire package. Individual serving packets can also be made or you may also just season individual portions and cook them directly over the coals without the wrapper.

Serves 8 to 10

1. Combine the fruit juices with the recado to make a soft paste.

2. Season the fish with salt and pepper and rub the paste all over the fish.

3. Toast the banana leaves to make them pliable (see page 19) and place them shiny side up on the counter.

4. Place the fish in the center of the banana leaves or foil, scatter the oregano or cilantro evenly over the fish and cover with the vegetables and chiles. Season with salt and pepper, and drizzle with the olive oil.

5. Wrap the banana leaves completely around the fish and tie with small strips of the leaf or foil to make a sealed package.

6. Place over hot coals or in a 400-degree-F oven and cook for about 15 minutes, turn over the package and cook 15 minutes more (only cook about 1/2 to 2/3 of this time for individual portions).

7. Turn back to the original position and cook 10 to 12 minutes more until the fish is done.

8. Open the package carefully and spoon some of the juices that form from cooking over the fish. Serve with warm corn tortillas and several salsas to make tacos.

Mac-Cum de Pescado
Fish Baked in a Pot

THIS COOKING METHOD FOR FISH has endured since pre-Columbian days but has richer, more complex flavors in its contemporary versions. In Campeche, the fish is wrapped in banana leaves after the spices are added and then placed in a clay pot or "Mac-Cum" and cooked on top of the fire. Here, we use the oven since the heat is more uniform and most of us do not have the proper pot for the original method. Either way produces a savory and moist fish that presents well.

Serves 4 to 6

1. Puree the recado with the lime juice, vinegar, cumin, oregano, black pepper, cloves, roasted garlic and roasted white onion.

(continued on page 181)

2 tablespoons Recado Colorado (see recipe on page 29)

1/4 cup lime juice

3 tablespoons mild vinegar

1/2 teaspoon cumin seed, toasted and ground

1 teaspoon Mexican oregano, toasted and ground

1 teaspoon ground black pepper

1/2 teaspoon ground cloves

6 cloves garlic, pan-roasted and peeled

1 medium white onion, peeled, sliced in 3 rounds and pan-roasted

Banana leaves or foil to wrap

Salt, to taste

2 to 2-1/2 pounds fresh fish filets (grouper, snapper, pompano, etc.) cut into 2-inch-wide strips

2 sweet peppers (green, red, yellow or mixed) charred, peeled, stemmed, seeded and cut into 1/2-inch strips

3 to 4 gueros, yellow hot chiles or 1 habanero, charred and left intact

2 medium tomatoes, cut into 8 wedges each

4 bay leaves, toasted

2. If using banana leaves, toast to make pliable (see page 19). Line a heavy casserole or roasting pan with the banana leaves or foil, place 1/2 of the recado mixture on the leaves in the center. Salt the fish filets, arrange on the recado and spread the remaining marinade on the top of the fish.

3. Place the roasted peppers, chiles, tomatoes, bay leaves and red onion on top along with the parsley and epazote. Drizzle with the oil and cover with more banana leaves or foil to make a sealed package.

4. Bake at 350 degrees F for 25 minutes, remove from the oven and let sit for a few minutes to steam before opening the package. This dish goes well with any rice dish or Budín de Chayote and Frijoles Colados Yucatecos (See recipes on pages 97 and 95).

5. You may leave the dish intact and let your guests serve themselves in traditional Maya style, or you may carefully remove the fish fillets and then spoon some of the vegetables and juices over the top for individual servings.

1 red onion, quartered, pan-toasted, then peeled and cut into 1/2-inch-wide strips

4 to 5 sprigs parsley or cilantro

2 to 3 sprigs epazote, oregano or marjoram

3 tablespoons olive or vegetable oil

Ceviche de Pulpo
Octopus Salad

2 quarts water

2 tablespoons sour orange juice
 OR 1 tablespoon mild vinegar

1-1/2 teaspoons salt

1 tablespoon Recado de Escabeche or
 de Bistec (see recipes on pages 32
 and 31)

1-1/2 to 2 pounds octopus

3/4 cup diced tomatoes

2/3 cup finely diced red onion,
 rinsed (see page 019)

1 or 2 jalapeño or serrano chiles,
 stemmed, seeded and finely
 minced

1/4 cup lime juice

1/3 cup chopped cilantro leaves

1/8 cup octopus cooking liquid,
 strained

2 tablespoons olive or vegetable oil

Black pepper and salt, to taste

1 teaspoon orange zest (optional)

ALTHOUGH THE NAME *CEVICHE* OFTEN describes a method of "cooking" seafood in citrus, in Mexico it also is used to describe previously cooked seafood, served chilled as a salad, employing the same ingredients and flavors as ceviche. In the many restaurants in Progresso, a Yucatán fishing village, many different ceviches are usually available; this one is popular during octopus season. This octopus salad is a great dish for lunch or light supper, as a small starter course or as an appetizer atop Totopos (see recipe on page 56).

Serves 4 as a main course

1. Heat the water, sour orange juice, salt and recado to boiling. Add the octopus and cook until tender (30 to 40 minutes for mature octopus; 10 to 15 for baby octopus).

2. Remove the octopus and cool. Peel off the outer skin. Discard. Cut the meat into bite-sized pieces.

3. Mix the octopus with the tomatoes, onion and chiles.

4. Whisk together the lime juice, cilantro and cooled cooking liquid. Add to the octopus and mix and toss.

5. Wait a few minutes; add the oil and toss again. Adjust for salt and pepper and garnish with the orange zest.

Desserts

UNTIL THE SPANISH ARRIVED in the New World, with sugarcane and honey bees, the Maya culture possessed no real tradition of desserts and sweets. At festive times, sweet syrups were probably made from the abundant native fruits and combined with nuts and seeds to create confections to satisfy the cravings for sweetness. Along with the Spanish and their penchant for sugary creations influenced by the Moors from North Africa came a profusion of ingredients from the east like cinnamon, cloves, new fruits, almonds and raisins, to name a few.

Modern-day Mayas, like the rest of their Mexican paisanos, revere sweets and desserts and, while they may not always consume them as part of the meal, sugary concoctions make up part of the daily diet and star during fiesta celebrations.

Queso Napolitano
Yucatán-Style Flan

1-1/4 cups sugar

1 (12-ounce) can evaporated milk

1 (14-ounce) can sweetened condensed milk or dulce de leche

6 whole eggs + 2 egg yolks

2 teaspoons Mexican or other premium vanilla extract

Dash salt

SIMILAR TO THE SPANISH-INFLUENCED FLAN but made with condensed rather than fresh milk, Queso Napolitano's name implies an Italian origin even if that heritage is somewhat in doubt. Rather than actual cheese, queso refers to the rich, thick texture of this flan, although, these days some cooks will add some cream cheese or *requeson* (ricotta-like cheese) to make it even more rich and creamy. If you want, add about 8 ounces cream cheese or Ricotta blended in with the milk and eggs in this recipe. You may also substitute one (13-ounce) can of coconut milk for the evaporated milk for a tasty variation. This is one of the most popular desserts around the Yucatán peninsula.

Makes about 8 servings

1. In a heavy saucepan or skillet (not nonstick), melt the sugar over medium heat until uniformly golden brown and smooth.

NOTE: *Move the sugar around the pan by tilting it rather than using a spoon to stir. This will help prevent recrystallization due to cool air mixing with the sugar.*

2. Pour the melted sugar into an 8-inch pie pan, 9-inch square pan or into individual, oven-proof custard cups.

3. Blend the remaining ingredients until smooth, then pour in the pan over the caramelized sugar.

4. Place the pan inside a larger pan with enough hot water to reach 1/2 the depth of the pan with the custard.

5. Bake at 350 degrees F for 45 minutes for one pan and 35 minutes for individual cups.

6. Remove from the pan with the water and cool at room temperature. Place a serving plate over the top of the pan and invert to unmold.

7. Cut into individual serving pieces and spoon some of the caramel over each piece.

Dulce de Papaya
Sweet Papaya Compote

A SIMPLE, YET QUITE DELICIOUS DESSERT made with fresh Mexican papaya, either green or ripe. Some cooks will soak the fruit in a mix of water and lime mineral (the same as used for treating corn) before cooking to firm up the papaya, although it is not absolutely necessary unless you prefer a chewier texture. Similar to the method of preparing sweet pumpkin or squash in other parts of Mexico called *en Tacha*, the Dulce de Papaya is usually scented with cinnamon, cloves and vanilla and some cooks also use fig leaves for flavor; however, you may also just serve it plain and enjoy the pure taste of the papaya. The finished product is often served with cubes of Dutch cheese or Crema Agria (recipe follows) to play against the cloying sweetness.

Serves 6 to 8

1 quart water

1-1/2 cups sugar

1/2 cup honey

1 Mexican papaya (about 4 to 5 pounds) peeled, seeded and cut into 2-inch pieces

2 (2-inch) sticks canela

4 or 5 whole cloves (optional)

Several large pieces orange, lemon or lime zest (optional)

2 teaspoons vanilla extract OR 1/2 vanilla bean, cut in half lengthwise

1. Put water, sugar and honey together in a heavy pot and bring to a boil. Cook until the sugar dissolves, then add the remaining ingredients and reduce to low heat.

2. Cook uncovered for about 1-1/2 hours until most of the syrup is absorbed and the remainder is fairly thick. Cool, then remove the canela, cloves and zest.

3. Serve the papaya with some of the syrup and cheese or Crema Agria.

CREMA AGRIA

Mexican Sour Cream

Make about 1 pint

1 pint heavy cream (if you can find cream that is not ultra-pasteurized, it will perform better)

5 tablespoons cultured buttermilk

1. Mix together, cover and allow to sit at room temperature for 24 hours. (The top of the refrigerator works well as it is a little warmer there.)

2. Stir and refrigerate.

NOTE: *This keeps well for several weeks. You may need to add more cream or some milk to thin it after a while as the Crema continues to culture as it sits.*

Pastelitos de Naranja
Orange-Cream Muffins

For the Cream Filling

1 (5-ounce) can sweetened condensed milk

1 cup orange juice

2 tablespoons lime juice

2 tablespoons sugar

2 egg yolks

2 tablespoons butter

For the Batter

1-1/4 cups sugar

1/2 cup butter

3 eggs, separated

1 teaspoon vanilla extract

1 tablespoon orange zest, very finely minced

3/4 cup orange juice

1-2/3 cups all-purpose flour

1/2 teaspoon salt

1 teaspoon baking powder

1/2 teaspoon baking soda

1/3 cup toasted, sliced almonds

For the Glaze

1/4 cup honey

1/4 cup orange juice

2 tablespoons butter

MANY VERSIONS OF THIS POPULAR CAKE are offered at *panaderías* (bakeries) around the Yucatán, at times in the form of muffins and other times as a layered cake. Sweet oranges give the cake a bit of a different flavor than sour oranges, like you would find there, yet I prefer it this way. Serve for breakfast, brunch or as a dessert.

Makes 12 large muffins

For the Cream Filling

1. Combine all but the butter and cook in a double boiler while stirring for 15 minutes. Remove from the heat.

2. Stir in the butter and set aside.

For the Batter

1. Cream the sugar and the butter with a mixer. Add the egg yolks one at a time and beat until fluffy. Add the extract, zest and juice and mix until well combined.

2. Beat the egg whites until medium stiff peaks form.

3. Sift together the flour, salt, baking powder and soda, then fold into the egg-butter mixture alternately with the beaten egg whites until a smooth, light batter is formed.

4. Line a muffin tin with paper muffin cups or grease well. Pour batter in each cup to 1/3 full. Place 2 tablespoons of the cream filling in each cup and top with the remaining batter. Sprinkle with the toasted almonds and bake at 375 degrees F for 18 to 20 minutes.

For the Glaze

1. Heat the honey and orange juice in a saucepan and boil for 5 minutes. Remove from heat and whisk in the butter.

2. Brush the tops of the muffins with the glaze and return to the oven for 5 more minutes. Cool and remove from the pan.

Fried Plantains

FRIED PLANTAINS ARE USED PLAIN as an accompaniment to soups, stews and other spicy dishes; as a breakfast item when drizzled with Crema Agria (see recipe for Dulce de Papaya on page 189); or as a sweet when sprinkled with cinnamon and sugar. Green plantains are firmer and less sweet, yellow are the most commonly used, and ones that are beginning to blacken are the sweetest, yet are a little more difficult to cook without turning them into a mush. The choice is yours. The double frying creates a crisper, less greasy surface on the plantain.

1. Peel and slice the plantain, either crosswise or lengthwise.

2. Fry in 350-degree F oil (deep enough to cover), a few slices at a time for 2 to 3 minutes.

3. Drain and cool for a few minutes.

4. Fry again for 3 to 4 minutes or until golden brown. Drain well and serve hot.

Plantains as desired for the number of servings (a large plantain can serve about 2)

Vegetable oil for frying

Dulce de Pepitas-Ha T'sikil Kab
Pumpkinseed Brittle

2-1/2 cups pumpkinseeds, toasted

1/2 teaspoon salt

1-1/4 cups honey (raw honey has better flavor)

3 tablespoons corn syrup

YOU WILL FIND THESE DELICIOUS crunchy-sweet candies for sale by street vendors and merchants in the mercados from high in the mountains in San Cristobal de las Casas, Chiapas, to the lowland cities of Villahermosa, Tabasco; Campeche, Campeche; and Merida, Yucatán. The addition of the corn syrup helps the honey bind the seeds better, but you can omit it also with good results.

Makes about 48 candies

1. Toss the seeds with the salt immediately after they are toasted.

2. Heat the honey and the corn syrup on medium heat in a heavy skillet until it foams and bubbles, then cook for about 5 minutes more while stirring.

3. Stir in the seeds and cook for 1 to 2 minutes more.

4. Drop by generous tablespoons on baker's parchment, silicon baking sheet or waxed paper. Press gently with the back of the spoon to flatten a bit.

5. Cool completely and cover for storage (do not refrigerate).

Poor Gentleman's "French" Toast Dessert

WITH MEDITERRANEAN ORIGINS, SIMILAR to Capirotada or bread pudding, Caballeros Pobres is a way of using day-old bread and transforming it into something special. Where French toast is usually served hot and topped with syrup, this dessert is cooked, then soaked in aromatic syrup, chilled and served later.

Serves 6 to 8

1. Mix the milks with the vanilla. Dip each slice of bread in the mixture to fully coat, then drain.

2. Beat the egg whites to a medium peak, adding 2 tablespoons sugar at the end. Fold in the egg yolks.

3. Heat a heavy skillet or griddle to medium high. In the pan, place enough oil to cover the bottom generously. Gently dip each soaked slice of bread in the egg whites to coat and then fry in the oil on both sides until golden brown. Drain on paper towels and cool.

4. In a heavy saucepan or skillet (not nonstick), melt the sugar over medium heat until uniformly golden brown and smooth. Move the sugar around the pan by tilting it rather than using a spoon to stir. Carefully add the water, canela and cloves and bring to a full boil. Reduce the heat to a slow boil and cook until the sugar has dissolved and the mixture has thickened to a syrup consistency. Remove from the heat, strain, and then add the raisins and almonds.

5. Dip each slice of bread in the syrup and place on a serving platter. Pour the remaining syrup and the raisins and almonds over the bread slices. Cover and refrigerate for several hours or overnight.

6. Serve with whipped cream, yogurt or Crema Agria (see recipe on page 189).

3/4 cup milk

1 (5-ounce) can sweetened condensed milk or dulce de leche

1 tablespoon Mexican or other premium vanilla extract

1 loaf French or other crusty bread, sliced diagonally, 3/4 to 1 inch thick

5 egg whites

2 tablespoons sugar

2 egg yolks, well beaten

Vegetable oil

2 cups sugar

2 cups water

2 (2-inch) sticks canela

1/2 teaspoon whole cloves

1/3 cup raisins or currants

1/3 cup slivered almonds, toasted (optional)

Lime Sherbet

7 cups water, 7 cups milk Or 4 cups
   milk and 3 cups evaporated milk

2-1/2 cups sugar

Dash salt

1 cup lime juice

1-1/2 tablespoons grated lime zest

SORBETE IS OFTEN THE PERFECT finale to a flavorful feast. The tangy fruit flavor and relative lightness of this dessert, especially when prepared as an ice, satisfies yet it is not overfilling. Sorbetes are popular all around Maya country, whether purchased from a shop, street vendor or made at home. I have included a variation using strawberries and you can also substitute other fruits. You have the choice of using water for an ice or milk for a richer sherbet.

Makes 2 quarts

1. Heat the water or milk with the sugar and salt until the sugar dissolves. Cool completely.

2. Mix in the lime juice and zest.

3. Freeze in trays or in an ice cream or sorbet machine.

NOTE: *For Strawberry Sherbet (Sorbete de Fresas), replace 2 cups of the water or milk with 2-1/2 cups of pureed and strained strawberries (unsweetened if using frozen strawberries) and reduce the lime juice to 1/3 cup.*

Crema de Mango con Ron
Mango-Rum Cream

I CREATED THIS DESSERT AT THE LAST MINUTE when I was preparing a feast for some local luminaries in Ocosingo, Chiapas. I was under pressure to prove that the visiting "Gringo" knew what he was doing in a Mexican kitchen, and being preoccupied with the main part of the meal, I completely neglected to plan a dessert. When Cecilia, the cook that was assisting, pointed out this oversight, I had to scramble to produce something impressive, and quickly. The ovens in the kitchen were malfunctioning so it limited our options. Recalling that there was an unused bag of small, sweet, yellow Manila mangoes that we had not used in the salad as previously planned, I whipped up this simple and tasty concoction. The wow factor of this dessert almost surpassed the dishes that we had slaved over for hours. Triple the rum and add a cup of milk and you can serve it as a cocktail, tropical eggnog, if you will.

8 Servings

1. Mix the egg yolks with the evaporated milk and cook in a double boiler for 12 to 15 minutes, stirring steadily. Place in a blender and allow to cool for a few minutes.

2. Add all the other ingredients, except the garnish, to the blender and puree smooth.

3. Place in serving cups or dishes and chill.

4. Sprinkle with the garnish before serving.

3 egg yolks

1 (12-ounce) can evaporated milk

1-1/2 pounds sweet, ripe mango, peeled and seeded

1 (14-ounce) can sweetened condensed milk

3/4 cup whipping cream or half-and-half

Juice of 1 sweet orange (about 1/2 cup)

1/2 teaspoon vanilla extract

1/2 cup dark or añejo rum

Ground canela, allspice and cloves for garnish

Torta de Cielo
Heavenly Almond Torte

12 ounces blanched, peeled almonds

2 tablespoons sugar

2 tablespoons all-purpose flour

1/2 teaspoon salt

1/2 teaspoon baking powder

10 eggs, separated

1-1/4 cups sugar

2 teaspoons vanilla extract

1/2 teaspoon almond extract
(optional)

1 tablespoon dark rum or brandy

1/2 teaspoon cream of tartar

THIS IS A CELEBRATION CAKE in the Yucatán. It utilizes ground almonds rather than flour for its structure and is not usually iced or filled. The torta is rich from the almonds yet relatively low fat, is not cloyingly sweet and keeps for several days.

Serves 8 to 10

1. Grind the almonds very fine with 2 tablespoons of sugar. Mix well with the flour, salt and baking powder.

2. Beat the egg yolks with the 1-1/4 cups sugar until light and creamy. Add the extracts, rum and flour-almond mixture and beat until smooth.

3. Whip the egg whites with the cream of tartar until medium-stiff peaks are formed.

4. By hand, gently beat in 1/3 of the egg whites into the egg yolk-almond-flour batter to lighten the batter. Gently fold in the remaining egg whites until they are just mixed in; do not overmix.

5. Well grease a 9- or 10-inch-diameter springform pan and pour the batter in.

6. Bake at 350 degrees F for 35 to 40 minutes until the cake is golden brown and beginning to pull away from the sides of the pan.

7. Cool for 10 to 15 minutes, remove from the pan and garnish with powdered sugar, toasted almonds and fruit, like sliced strawberries or mango.

Mermelada de Papaya
Papaya Marmalade

2 to 2-1/2 pounds Mexican (pink) papayas, peeled, seeded and cubed

1-1/2 cups water

1-1/4 cups sugar

1/3 cup lime juice

1 tablespoon lime zest, made in thin strips with a zester tool or minced fine

2 tablespoons orange zest, made in thin strips with a zester tool or minced fine

THIS EASY-TO-PREPARE FRUIT MARMALADE is a morning favorite around the Yucatán peninsula on *molletes* (toasted crusty rolls), along with a cup of coffee or hot chocolate. It also makes a great sweet filling for pastries or a glaze for chicken or pork in contemporary Maya cooking. The recipe is easily doubled and put in canning jars, although it will keep in the refrigerator for several months without canning.

Makes about 24 ounces

1. Puree the papaya with the water until smooth.

2. Combine with the sugar and lime juice in a heavy pot or saucepan, then bring to a full boil. Reduce the heat to just boiling and, stirring constantly, cook until the mixture reaches the "soft ball" stage, 235 degrees F.

3. Stir in the zests and cook for 1 more minute.

4. Transfer the marmalade to a cool receptacle to stop the cooking process, cool to room temperature or place in canning jars and proceed with the steps for safe canning using a hot water bath.

Beverages

SOME OF THE BEVERAGES CONSUMED in the Maya world today include traditional Atole and Pinole made from corn for many centuries, fruit Licuados and Aguas, Spanish-influenced Horchata, fermented Tepache and Cocktails, reportedly first named so in Campeche after the *Cola de Gallo* (rooster's tail).

Horchata
Rice Refresher

1-1/2 cups white rice

1 quart water

1/2 cup skinned almonds

3/4 cup water

2 teaspoons ground canela

2/3 cup sugar

2 quarts water, divided

HORCHATA IS ENJOYED IN the Maya lands as well as throughout Mexico. It was brought to the New World by the Spanish and is now almost a Mexican national drink. Frothy, creamy and rich without any dairy products, Horchata is normally served chilled although I have had great success in gently heating it and serving it hot during cool weather.

Makes about 2 quarts

1. Soak the rice in 1 quart of water overnight. Soak the almonds in 3/4 cup of water overnight.

2. Drain the rice and the almonds and grind separately as fine as possible.

3. Combine the ground rice, almonds, canela and sugar with 1 quart of water and blend thoroughly. Strain into a container and mix in the other quart of water. Chill and serve over ice or blend with ice for a frozen drink.

HORCHATA DE COCO

COCONUT IS ALSO OFTEN added to horchata in many tropical areas. To make this variation, follow the previous Horchata recipe, reducing the almonds to 1/4 cup, the sugar to 1/2 cup and adding 2/3 cup of sweetened, shredded coconut. Blend the coconut with the other ingredients in step 3 before straining and proceed.

Tepache
Fermented Pineapple Beverage

AT MY FIRST ENCOUNTER WITH this drink in a mercado, it was like nothing I had tasted before—cool and refreshing, slightly sweet and fruity with a little spritz of carbonation and barely a hint of alcohol. Easy to make if you have a container and the space to keep it, Tepache is a perfect beverage for a summertime outdoor fiesta. The procedure is a lot like making pineapple vinegar. Tepache is purported to originate in Mexico State, however it is widely available and popular in most locations in the Maya world.

Makes 1-3/4 gallons

1. Cut the tops off the pineapples (leave the skin on), rinse well and cut into eighths lengthwise.

2. If using piloncillo, heat with 1 cup of the water until dissolved. Cool.

3. Place the pineapple, sugar and spices in a glass or nonreactive metal container with 1 gallon of the water. Mix well to dissolve the sugar.

4. Leave uncovered for 2 hours, then cover (not too tightly) and let sit for 48 to 72 hours at room temperature. You should begin to see some activity.

5. Strain the liquid and return to the container along with the rest of the water and the beer if you are using it.

6. Cover and let sit for 24 to 48 hours more.

7. Taste and add more water or beer to achieve the desired sweetness. (The Tepache should be a little carbonated and sweet but not cloyingly so.)

8. Refrigerate to store and serve cold over ice.

2 medium pineapples, at least 3 pounds total, ripe

1-3/4 pounds piloncillo or light brown or raw sugar

1-1/2 gallons water

2 sticks canela

1 teaspoon lightly toasted allspice berries

4 to 5 whole cloves (optional)

1 (12-ounce) bottle beer, bottle conditioned ales work best, but any beer that is not too dark will do (optional)

Aguas Frescas
Fresh Fruit Beverages

AGUAS FRESCAS, FRESH WATERS, ARE ALSO OFTEN CALLED *aguas frutas* or simply *aguas*. They are lighter, hence more refreshing than pure fruit juices. They can be made with just about any fruit, melon or combination that you like. The only adjustment is the amount of sweetener depending on the variety or ripeness of the fruit. Another variation is to replace half of the water in the recipe with sparkling or carbonated water. A refreshing cooler by itself, Agua Fresca is a perfect accompaniment to Maya meals.

Makes about 2 quarts

1. Puree the fruit with the Simple Syrup and lime juice.

2. Mix with the water (strain if desired) and chill.

3. Serve over ice and garnish with fruit slices and mint.

SIMPLE SYRUP

COMBINE EQUAL PARTS of sugar and water, bring to a boil and cook for 5 minutes, stirring occasionally. Cool before using. May be stored covered in the refrigerator for several weeks.

4 cups melon, pineapple, strawberries, mango, papaya or other fruits OR 2 cups of freshly squeezed orange or grapefruit juice OR 3/4 pound tamarind paste

1/3 to 1/2 cup or more to taste, Simple Syrup (recipe follows)

1/4 cup lime or lemon juice

1-3/4 quarts cool water

Atoles

1 quart water

Dash salt

Aromatic flavorings, if desired

1/2 pound fresh masa, Fresh Masa
    Substitute (see recipe on page 73)
    OR 3/4 cup masa harina mixed
    with 1/2 cup warm water

Sugar to sweeten, as desired (1/4 to
    1/2 cup is typical)

Aromatics (may be used individually
    or combined)

3 to 4 lime or orange leaves or the
    zest of 1 lime or orange

2 teaspoons whole allspice berries,
    lightly cracked

1 (2- to 3-inch) stick canela

1/2 teaspoon whole cloves

ATOLE IS A TYPE OF COOKED corn beverage that is like gruel. It is often consumed in the morning, and in the more remote villages it may constitute a full breakfast when served along with a few tortillas. This nutritious and satisfying drink has been consumed since long before the Spanish arrived, although the addition of canela and sugar has made it more palatable for western tastes. In traditional Maya cookery, there are hundreds of atoles, each containing subtle distinctions. Here, I am including a few of the most common and you can use your imagination to create your own variation.

ATOLE DE MASA

Maya Corn Beverage

THIS IS THE BASIC ATOLE recipe used all around Maya territory. Many flavorings may be added (suggestions are listed after the recipe) or it may be consumed plain or just sweetened with a little sugar. To make Chileatole, simply add the strained puree of toasted and soaked chiles or coarsely chopped, dry chiles (see page 23) until you reach the spiciness that you like.

Makes 4 to 6 servings

1. Bring the water and salt to a boil with any of the aromatics that you are using. Cook for 5 minutes and strain.

2. Mix the masa with 2-1/2 cups of the water until smooth, then mix into the remaining water.

3. Bring to a slow boil and cook, stirring constantly, until thickened (about 10 minutes).

4. Serve immediately.

ATOLE CON PEPITA

ANOTHER COMMON INGREDIENT in Atole is pumpkinseed. The seeds add an interesting flavor and essential fats and protein. Mix 3/4 cup of toasted and finely ground pumpkinseeds with 1 cup of boiling water. Add this paste to the atole in step 2 on page 208 and proceed.

Chorreado
Maya Chocolate Drink

1/2 pound white rice or fresh masa or Fresh Masa Substitute (see recipe on page 73) OR 1/4 pound of each

1 pint water (for soaking rice)

3 rounds (10 ounces) Mexican chocolate

2 tablespoons lightly toasted and ground anise seed

1 tablespoon ground canela

1-3/4 cups sugar

1-1/2 quarts water, divided

THIS ATOLE-LIKE DRINK is also similar to Horchata as it uses rice. It may also be made with masa or a combination of the two to make a thicker beverage. The chocolate adds a smooth richness to this ancient concoction.

Makes 6 to 8 servings

1. Soak the rice (if using) in 1 pint of water overnight.

2. Strain the rice and discard the water from soaking. Combine the rice and/or masa, chocolate, anise, canela and sugar with 3/4 quart of water, blend smooth and strain with a fine mesh strainer or cheesecloth.

3. Heat the remaining 3/4 quart of water and keep warm on the side.

4. Heat the strained mixture, stirring constantly, to a gentle boil and cook until thickened (about 5 minutes).

5. Slowly stir in the remaining warm water until a smooth, fairly thin consistency is achieved (the mixture will thicken when cooled).

6. Chill and serve with a little ground cinnamon and/or chocolate to garnish.

Pinole (K'A)
Toasted Corn Drink

PINOLE IS A BEVERAGE that is made from toasted kernels of corn and may be served mixed with cold water or cooked with water to make a thicker atole. The dry portion of this recipe may be prepared in advance to have an "instant" mix on hand.

Makes 4 to 6 servings

1. Toast the corn kernels in a heavy pan over medium heat until uniformly golden brown and beginning to smell like popcorn. Remove the corn from the pan and cool.

2. Grind the corn as fine as possible and mix with the remaining ingredients.

3. For cold drinks: Blend 2 tablespoons of the dry mixture with 8 ounces of cold water and serve over ice with a squeeze of lime or orange.

4. For hot drinks: Heat 1 quart of water to boiling, slowly stir in the dry mix and simmer, stirring constantly for 6 to 8 minutes.

1 pound dried corn kernels or dry posole

1 tablespoon ground canela

1 teaspoon ground allspice

Pinch ground cloves (optional)

2/3 to 3/4 cup sugar

Yucatán Sunshine

XTABENTUN IS AN ANISE- and honey-flavored liquor made from a flowering plant from the Yucatán known by the same name. If you do not have any on hand, you may substitute Pernod, Anisette, Ouzo or Galliano with good results.

Makes 4 generous cocktails

1. Combine the juice, tequila, Xtabentun and the ice. Shake or stir vigorously and strain into cocktail glasses.

2. Float some grenadine on top and garnish with orange slices. Enjoy!

2-1/2 cups (20 ounces) orange or mango juice, or a mix of the two

6 to 8 ounces premium tequila or mezcal

4 ounces Xtabentun or substitute

2 cups ice

Grenadine and orange slices to garnish (optional)

Food and Cooking Travel Adventures in Mexico with Daniel Hoyer

www.welleatenpath.com

Ingredient and equipment sources

This list is constantly changing and growing. There are an increasing number of sources for the ingredients called for in this book. First, check your local supermarket, farmer's market and Latin American/Mexican tienda or store.

SANTA FE SCHOOL OF COOKING

116 West San Francisco Street
Santa Fe, NM 87501
cookin@santafeschoolofcooking.com
505-983-4511
http://santafeschoolofcooking.com/
Ingredients, equipment and utensils. Cooking classes
  (Daniel teaches here)

BURNS FARMS

1345 Bay Lake Loop
Groveland, FL 34736
352-429-4048
Fresh hoja santa (acuyo) in season

THE CMC COMPANY

P.O. Drawer 322
Avalon, NJ 08202
800-CMC-2780; fax 609-861-3065
www.thecmccompany.com
Large selection of Mexican ingredients and equipment

GOURMET SLEUTH

www.gourmetsleuth.com
408-354-8281
Mexican and other ingredients and equipment

MEX GROCER

www.mexgrocer.com
Many Mexican ingredients and equipment

MELISSA'S

800-468-7111
Fresh and dried chiles, corn husks, tomatillos
  and other necessities

DON ALFONSO FOODS

800-456-6100
Chiles, prepared moles, etc.

Frieda's by Mail

4465 Corporate Center Drive
Los Alamitos, CA 90720
800-421-9477
www.friedas.com
Fresh and dried chiles

Herbs of Mexico

3903 Whittier Boulevard
Los Angeles, CA 90023
213-261-2521
Dried herbs and spices, such as epazote

Kitchen Market

218 Eighth Avenue
New York, NY 10011
212-243-4433; fax 888-hot-4433
www.kitchenmarket.com
Canela, Mexican oregano, avocado leaves, etc.

Generation Farms

1109 North McKinney
Rice, TX 75155
903-326-4263; fax 903-326-6511
www.generationfarms.com
Fresh epazote and hoja santa (1/2 pound minimum, but
    1/4 pound if you order several herbs)

Penzey's Ltd.

933 Muskego
Brookfield, WI 53150
800-741-7787; fax 262-679-7878
www.penzeys.com
Canela, dried epazote, Mexican oregano, and
    chipotle chiles

Valley Food Warehouse

14530 Nordhoff
Panorama City, CA 91402
818-891-9939; fax 818-891-1781
Avocado leaves, epazote and banana leaves, as well as
    other Mexican and Central American ingredients

Plaza Piaxtla

898 Flushing Avenue
Brooklyn, NY 11206
718-386-2626
Good source for equipment and Mexican ingredients
    including fresh epazote and dried hoja santa

Stop 1 Supermarket

210 W. 94th Street
New York, NY 10025
212-864-9456
Large selection of Mexican chiles and seasonings including
    dried avocado leaves, hoja santa, epazote, and canela

Photo Credits

Index

Metric Conversion Chart

Liquid and Dry Measures

U.S.	Canadian	Australian
¼ teaspoon	1 mL	1 ml
½ teaspoon	2 mL	2 ml
1 teaspoon	5 mL	5 ml
1 tablespoon	15 mL	20 ml
¼ cup	50 mL	60 ml
⅓ cup	75 mL	80 ml
½ cup	125 mL	125 ml
⅔ cup	150 mL	170 ml
¾ cup	175 mL	190 ml
1 cup	250 mL	250 ml
1 quart	1 liter	1 litre

Temperature Conversion Chart

Fahrenheit	Celsius
250	120
275	140
300	150
325	160
350	180
375	190
400	200
425	220
450	230
475	240
500	260